THE PARADOXES OF INDIA'S POLITICS

THE PARADOXES OF INDIA'S POLITICS

PRAFULL GORADIA

Vitasta
LET KNOWLEDGE SPREAD

Published by
Renu Kaul Verma
Vitasta Publishing Pvt Ltd
2/15, Ansari Road, Daryaganj
New Delhi - 110 002
info@vitastapublishing.com

ISBN 978-93-86473-58-5

First Edition 2019
MRP ₹ 750

Cover and layout by Somesh Kumar Mishra
Printed by Vikas Computer and Printers

Contents

Why this Book?

To portray the paradoxes in the different spheres of Indian life with a number of examples is the purpose of this book.

This volume begins with the most glaring contradiction at the very beginning of this nation's life as the country today called India, with defined boundaries, ephemeral concepts and confused politics. That Qaid-e-Azam Jinnah should strive for a Muslim homeland and, in the process, save the Hindu civilisation by creating the Hindu Bharat is the first of many such paradoxes that fill the nation's life.

That an armed Subhas Bose should help to precipitate the independence of India rather than Gandhi's sustained non-violence struggle and that Jawaharlal Nehru should become its first prime minister, and rule for 17 years, leaving behind a controversial legacy of leadership follow immediately after.

The country's first priority is economic development, said Prime Minister Nehru in 1947 but the people, industrialists and traders, who were proven performers, were, according to a speech Nehru made in 1942: 'In free India, corrupt and black marketeers will be hanged from the nearest lamp post.' This was paradoxical as a free-market trader was labled corrupt in the beholder's eye, ie. the Nehru government's eye. According to him, development was to be headed by the Planning Commission whereas history said, every country that adopted such a commission had its economy either drowned or languishing in the doldrums, as time has shown socialist economies to be.

Could these paradoxes be the results of the Indian ethos that has preferred the inspiration of *rishis* to innovate or invent rather than the empiricism that the Western world has invariably depended on? For example, the Indian or Hindu study of longevity called *Ayurveda* was initiated mainly by rishi Charak. He did not confine himself to medicine or the cure of illness or the relief from undesirable symptoms. Charak went much further and attended to making the healthy healthier. His imagination was that of a genius, but he did not consider it necessary to dissect the body before arriving at the ways to treat a digestive ailment or any problem of the alimentary canal. In contrast, a Western doctor might have spent years researching on any number of human systems before arriving at conclusions like the need for an enema. Wherever then an Indian recipe becomes outdated or its rishi makes a mistake, his conclusions or study falters.

Going further to a few more paradoxes, one relates to Akbar and Aurangzeb. The former was famous for tolerance and near impartiality between Hindus and Muslims. He initiated a new religion which he called Din-e-Ilahi, meaning a religion in praise of Allah. His courtiers explained that Akbar meant in praise of God and not specifically Allah. This is only one instance of the Badshah's doublespeak; there are critics who believe that he was altogether a deceptive ruler. He made a show of his impartiality to keep the Hindus on his side; they were the overwhelmingly larger portion of his subjects. In short, he was misleading his people for the sake of his power. Whereas Aurangzeb was openly and candidly an orthodox Muslim without any sympathy for Hindus; they knew where they stood in the eyes of their emperor. Which would you prefer? Better to be disliked than to be deceived! But paradoxically we call Akbar, The Great and Aurangzeb cruel. These and many other paradoxes in our political life has egged me on to write this present discourse on paradoxes.

NATION VERSUS MINORITY

VOTE BANK VERSUS COMPULSORY VOTING

VOTING FOR all parliamentary and assembly elections should be made compulsory by amending the Representation of the People Act. Such a reform is likely to go a long way in electing competent representatives as opposed to just those standing as candidates. Most importantly, what has come to be called as vote-bank politics would cease to exist. Neither political parties nor candidates will be able to pamper any section of the people because up to 95 per cent of the electorate would have to participate. This writer has been observing elections in Ahmedabad and has heard a number of political workers say that by and large, the local Muslims vote solidly for their favourite party – that is, up to 90 per cent of them or even more. This effectively means that a Muslim vote is worth two votes of other communities.

If this phenomenon is true for the entire country, this explains why several parties in the country have pro-minority programmes. The high-water mark of such an agenda was exemplified by former Prime Minister Manmohan Singh, who openly declared that Muslims have the first right and that 15 per cent of the country's resources would be first earmarked for them. Having been a refugee from West Pakistan, he surely had no personal bias and was doing so for electoral benefit.

Moreover, the importance of voting in general elections is not realised widely enough. Citizens consider the exercise unimportant if not a waste of time, especially when they see a long queue outside the polling booth. 'How is my vote going to make any difference?' is a question not infrequently on the lips of even an educated citizen. Arguments like 'numbers are with the masses; classes do not matter', etc. are frequently made. In the long run, for a democracy to flourish, *the will to vote* and elect the best possible government should be on everyone's mind.

After all, a government run by elected politicians is the engine of society. Politics should not be ignored by those who have access to more secure and lucrative careers. In fact, ideally, the country's most talented citizens should run its government. And traditional families or dynasties or the unemployable youth must not monopolise the pursuit of public life. Compulsory voting will help induce awareness of these factors and their importance.

There was a time, not so long ago, when more than 55 per cent of the votes cast were considered satisfactory. In the 2004 general poll, less than 49 per cent people voted. If voting in any constituency or a section was far more prolific, suspicions were voiced that there could have been booth capturing. Anything like 80 per cent caused electoral authorities to order a re-poll in such booths. Alternatively, provocative circumstances resulted in enthusiastic voting. For example, in the 2014 general election, people voted briskly (66.38 per cent) because of charges of corruption against the Manmohan Singh government as well as the UPA's blatant Muslim pampering.

Imagine, in the 2014 general elections, our country was rewarded with a government with an overall majority after a break of 30 years! The highest percentage of voting recorded was at 66.38 per cent in 2014. In this writer's years in Kolkata, he witnessed how cadre-based parties managed electoral roles. Outside every big *basti* of the metropolis, during the season of intensive revision of rolls, were stationed a couple of trusted party men. When young Election Commission surveyors, employed temporarily on a daily basis, appeared for population surveys in the bastis, the party men gently enquired as to what they were looking for. The relatively innocent surveyors declared their mission. In response, the party staff offered a ready-made list of adults in the basti. The surveyors were free to make use of the list for making the revised rolls. I suspect that most youngsters having to move around in the sultry weather blindly copied the ready lists. Only such organised manipulation explains the mysteries of Kolkata's predictable electoral behaviour for three decades until 2011.

Compulsory voting should be a necessary change for our citizens; its introduction would help facilitate a countrywide awareness about the importance of voting. Such a mandatory provision of law would also ensure the need to register oneself on the electoral roll. At present, whoever gets recorded through the intensive revision by a surveyor visit to one's residence becomes enrolled as a voter. Very few new potential voters go to the sub-divisional office to get themselves enrolled. Hardly any old voter goes on his own initiative to check whether his name is safely still on the roll. There is a huge job-related migration in India today. As enrollment is based on local addresses, a large chunk of the working population is left out of the voting in every election. The State electoral office usually takes no initiative to keep the roll up to date. On the other hand, there is even less activity when a summary revision is ordered in preparation of an upcoming election. Compulsory voting would wake up all concerned. If anyone happens to have applied and he still finds his name missing, the responsibility will be of the government's.

There is nothing new or original about making voting compulsory. In Australia, it was introduced first in 1915 in Queensland and over time, caught on in the other federating States. By now only about five per cent of the enrolled voters fail to cast their votes. People in this situation are asked to explain their failure to vote. If no satisfactory reason is provided (for example, illness or religious prohibition) a fine of up to $170 is imposed, and failure to pay the fine may result in a court hearing and additional costs.

The immediate justification for compulsory voting at the federal level was the low voter turnout (59.38 per cent) for the 1922 federal election, which went down from 71.59 per cent in the 1919 federal election. Compulsory polling is never on the agenda of any government or political party in any country. In Australia, the actual initiative for change was made by one Herbert Payne, a backbench Tasmanian senator, who on 16 July 1924 introduced a private member's Bill in the Senate. Payne's Bill was passed with little debate – no votes were recorded against the Bill. It received royal assent on 31 July 1924 as the Commonwealth Electoral Act 1924. The 1925 federal election was the first to be conducted under compulsory voting which saw the turnout figure rise to 91.4 per cent. The turnout increased to about 95 per cent within a couple of elections and has stayed at about that level since, ie. for the next hundred years almost.

In India a voter might be allowed to inform the local electoral officer, say a fortnight in advance why he/she will be unable to cast his/her vote. If s/he fails to do so for any emergent reason, he may convey his regret, with reason, within a fortnight after the polling date. If the excuse is accepted, well and good; if not, he should be fined Rs100.

Paradoxically, India is a parliamentary democracy where elected leaders rule, but voting is not compulsory here, nor the number of candidates contesting for a seat limited. So here is a situation in which, if there are a hundred votes in a community, only 20 people may vote and a candid who gets just 7 votes may be the winner, even when just 3 candidates have contested. India therefore needs compulsory voting.

ALL OTHERS VS HINDUS

EVEN AFTER the creation of Pakistan, Hindustan is not free of the communal question. The only way to make the country homogeneous is by arranging for an exchange of population.

While presiding over the Muslim League session in Lahore in March 1940, Mohammed Ali Jinnah declared that Muslims are not a minority but a nation by any definition. This was the crux of his two-nation theory which succeeded in his achieving a homeland for the Muslims. He had in mind a maximal migration of his community to the new homeland.

For those of them who could not possibly do so, he endorsed President Rajendra Prasad's proposal that they could remain in India but *as aliens* on the basis of visas issued by the Government of India. In the former President's words, 'the Muslims in Hindustan will have the status of foreigners and, therefore, be subject to the same disability that a foreigner suffers from'. Jinnah reacted by observing that 'the Muslims who are citizens of India today will, after Partition, cease to be citizens of Hindustan' and among his choices would be as proposed by Rajendra Prasad.

These contentions of the two leaders gave a burial to the concept of minority which had been propounded by reformist Sir Syed Ahmad Khan in the last quarter of the 19th century. He campaigned for separate nominations for the Muslims to the local self-government institutions that were created by Viceroy Lord Ripon. In 1906, a delegation of 35 Muslim eminences, led by Sir Aga Khan, met Viceroy Minto and demanded separate electorates and reservation in government jobs. Two months later, they established the All India Muslim League in order to follow up politically on their demands made to Lord Minto. The 1909 Morley-Minto Reforms implemented the demands.

Under the Morley-Minto Reforms of 1909, the Muslims obtained separate electorates. In 1916, under the Lucknow Pact signed by Bal Gangadhar Tilak and Jinnah, the Congress party had agreed to separate electorates as also weightage for Muslims on a scale higher than that provided under the Morley-Minto Reforms, both in the Central legislature as well as in provinces where they were in minority. The Pact of 1916 envisaged that Muslim representation across the country became about 30 per cent higher than their population.

For the Central Legislative Council, the percentage of Muslim representation was fixed at 33.3 per cent. After the conclusion of the Gandhi-Irwin Pact in 1931, Mahatma Gandhi went to London to attend the second session of the Round Table Conference. He failed to secure an agreed solution of the communal problem. According to Constitutional

Advisor VP Menon, the sole outcome of the second session was widening of the cleavage between the Congress and the minorities, especially the Muslim League. Prime Minister Ramsay MacDonald announced the Communal Award on 16 August 1932. It provided for separate electorates for Muslims, Europeans, Sikhs, Indian Christians, Anglo-Indians and the depressed classes. The total Muslim representation across the country under the Award was much in excess of their proportionate population.

The Communal Award left the Muslims of Bengal and Punjab in a strong position. They not only retained separate electorates but were also disproportionately given more seats in the provincial assemblies. Father of the Indian Constitution BR Ambedkar who comprehensively examined the Award and the Muslims at the Round Table Conference complained:

(i) That their representatives in the entire Provincial as well as in the Central Legislature should be elected by separate electorates.

(ii) That they should be allowed to retain weightage in representation given to Muslim minorities in those provinces in which they were a minority in the population, and that in addition, they should be given in those provinces where they were a majority such as the Punjab, Sind, North-West Frontier Province and Bengal, a guaranteed statutory majority of seats. The Award of His Majesty's Government settled this dispute by the simple, rough and ready method of giving the Muslims all that they wanted, without caring for the Hindu opposition.

The Award is iniquitous in as much as it accorded unequal treatment to the Hindu and Muslim minorities. It granted the Muslim minorities in the Hindu provinces the right of self-determination in the matter of electorates but it did not grant the same right to the Hindu minorities in Muslim provinces.

In the Hindu provinces, a Muslim minority was allowed to choose the kind of electorates it wanted and the Hindu majority was not permitted to have any say in that matter. But in the Muslim provinces, it was the Muslim majority which was allowed to choose the kind of electorate it preferred, and the Hindu minority was not permitted to have any say in the same. Thus, the Muslims in the Muslim provinces, having been given both statutory majority and separate electorates, the Award must be said to have imposed upon the Hindu minorities Muslim rule which they could neither alter nor influence.

This is what constitutes the fundamental wrong in the Communal Award. That this was a grave wrong must be admitted. For, it offends certain political principles which have now become axiomatic. As has been well said, 'If in any state there is a body of men who possess unlimited political power, those over whom they rule can never be free. For, the one assured result of historical investigation is the lesson that uncontrolled power is invariably poisonous to those who possess it. They are always tempted to impose their canon of good upon others, and in the end, they assume that the good of the community depends upon the continuance of their power. Liberty always demands a limitation of political authority….'

In the course of the Round Table Conferences 1930 to 1932, the Muslims extracted the maximum concessions as a minority, as the Prime Minister, Ramsay MacDonald, gave what is known as the Communal Award, which met all the Muslim demands. The final outcome was, to a great extent, conditioned by the pleadings of the then Viceroy, Lord Willingdon, who repeatedly emphasised that if the British wanted to safeguard their position in India, they had no option but to keep the Muslims satisfied, for they constituted the one reliable force in India on which the British could depend in stemming the rising tide of Indian nationalism.

The Communal Award, thus, represented a clear victory for the tactics adopted by founding member of the Unionist Party of the Punjab Fazl-i-Husain, and helped reinforce the traditional view of the dominant Muslim elite that their interests would be served better through friendship with Britain, than aligning with Indian nationalism (quoted from *Pathway to Pakistan* by Khaliq-uz-Zaman).

The concept of minority arose in Europe at the end of World War I when national territories were redrawn, and the population of a country came to be directed against its will by the war to another country so that the divided community needed safeguards to save it from ethnic extinction. In sharp contrast, the Indian Muslims forced Partition on their own demands, based on the two-nation theory. Furthermore, even after Partition, a large section of the community preferred to remain in Hindustan out of their choice.

It so happened that at the command of Mahatma Gandhi, Jawaharlal Nehru was made the Prime Minister, although democratically, the Congress wanted Sardar Vallabhbhai Patel. Nehru, therefore, needed to build his own base in the Congress.

He chose the Muslims as one major segment of this base. In order to favour them, he resurrected the concept of minority and gave its members special privileges in the Constitution, especially through Articles 25 to 30. In the bargain, Article 14, which insisted on equality before the law, was violated and reduced the majority of Indians to an unequal and inferior status.

These sops of Nehru gave the Congress a free hand to appease the Muslim community in order to ensure votes. The climax of this pampering was reached by former Prime Minister Manmohan Singh when he declared 15 per cent of the country's resources would first be assigned to the Muslims. The question that arose over Partition was the status of Muslims who would be left in Hindustan. The question that concerned the Hindus was: How far did the creation of Pakistan remove communal tension from Hindustan?

Paradoxically, it must be admitted that even with the creation of Pakistan, Hindustan is not free of the communal question. While Pakistan was made a homogeneous state by redrawing its boundaries, Hindustan remained a composite state. *Musalman*s are scattered all over Hindustan. The only way to make Hindustan homogeneous is to arrange for an exchange of population even now. Until that is done, even with the creation of Pakistan, the problem will remain in Hindustan just as before Partition and will continue to produce disharmony in the body politic of Hindustan.

LEAGUE ACCELERATED ASSAM MIGRATION

WHAT IS today the controversial National Register of Citizens, had its slow and scattered beginnings at the turn of the 19th into the 20th century. Assam's attraction was its plentiful land watered by several rivers, especially the mighty Brahmaputra. A number of rivers narrowed during the dry season exposing on their sides fertile margins which are locally called 'char' lands. These were unoccupied and there for the picking by immigrants who came from East Bengal, where there were too many residents for the limited land. As the population grew, gradually more migrants came into Assam. As they worked hard and accumulated surpluses, they could buy parcels of normal land from willing sellers. Until about 1937, there were few settlements of the East Bengali immigrants by design.

Under the Government of India Act of 1935, provincial governments were formed by political parties. Soon enough, a Sir Mohammed Saadulla of the Muslim League became the Premier. In the 1937 elections, the League led by Jinnah, was disappointed with its meagre winnings in UP, the largest province in undivided India. Talk of a distinctly separate Muslim holy land began in seriousness. The idea was first concretely mooted by the poet Iqbal who presided over the 1930 League session at Allahabad. A few years later, a Cambridge University scholar, Chaudhry Rehmat Ali worked out a theoretical note and innovated the name Pakistan, the land of the devout. Jinnah's idea was that five provinces should form the holy land, namely Assam, Bengal, North West Frontier, Punjab and Sind. Balochistan came in later.

From the Muslim majority angle, Assam appeared touch and go to Jinnah although the Hindu impression was that they had a clear majority. Premier Saadulla got down to the business of facilitating as many East Bengali Muslims to come across and settle in Assam. A parallel whispering campaign was started that the Adivasis were not really Hindus but worshipped animals or were Christian. There was thus a race to somehow prove that there were more Muslims in Assam than Hindus.

In the course of a discussion at Shillong in 1945, Viceroy Lord Wavell noted in his diary that while the reason for the encouragement of this migration was officially justified as being to grow more food, the real object was to grow more Mohammedans (as recorded by BK Nehru in his book *Nice Guys Finish Second*). The tale of illegal migrants into Assam is an old one told by all observers but swept under the carpet by the Congress party and its Muslim supporters. Other distinguished Muslims like Sheikh Mujibur Rahman and former Pakistan PM, Zulfikar Ali Bhutto, openly expressed the view that without Assam, the economy of East Pakistan could not be complete.

The Census Report of 1931 had recorded a rise of Muslim population due to migration from Mymensingh and East Bengal generally. Nevertheless, they comprised under 27 per cent. The 1941 Census Report showed that this figure had gone up to nearly 34 per cent. Immigration of East Bengali colonists was pouring in, a remark recorded by the Census Superintendent of Assam, CS Mullan, ICS. incidentally, by 1921, the cultivators from east Bengal had gone much beyond the southern districts and into central areas.

The entire episode is heart-rending for those who care for Assam. The writer has often visited the State and has seen all its tea growing sub-districts. I was there for some ten days during the 1983 elections, which were boycotted by those who loved Assam. In many of the assembly constituencies, the voting was pathetically low although the Hiteswar Saikia government had ensured perfect law and order. Most of the electoral officers in the heartland constituencies and the booths therein were manned by men flown in from other States. Yet, in one constituency the votes cast were only 268 and a large number did not cross a few hundred or thousand. The candidates were too frightened to campaign. Except for the then Bengali-speaking Cachar and Goalpara districts and possibly Barpeta, there was a total *bandh*. I spent those five days based in Guwahati and could not buy even a *bidi* or cigarette. One only saw birds and occasionally a rushing caravan of six to seven Ambassador cars filled with government officials. I could move about in my hired car with boldly printed labels of PRESS and a friend who posed as a photographer. The reported massacre in Nellie took place on the morrow of the voting day.

Quoting from the *Hindustan Standard*, a well-patronised Kolkata daily of the pre- and post-independence decades, Dr Rajendra Prasad in his book, *India Divided*, stated, 'It is sad but by no means improbable that in another 30 years, Sibsagar district will be the only part of Assam in which an Assamese will find himself at home.'

The Census Report of 1941 completes the story with a short but significant sentence quoted, 'The most noticeable rise in the Muslim population is in Assam and once again represents migration from Mymensingh and East Bengal generally.' This policy of colonisation of Assam by the Muslims of Bengal was continued under the joint auspices of the Muslim League ministries of Sir Saadullah in Assam and Sir Nazimuddin in Bengal, as the following Bengal Government communique published in the press, in the last week of October 1944, shows. It goes on to quote the Census Report of 1941: The Government of Assam in their resolution dated the 21st June 1940 prohibited settlement of land with persons coming from outside the province after 1st January, 1938. The Bengal Legislative Council went on to appeal to the Governor to ask for the Viceroy's intervention in Assam.

Rajendra Prasad quoted a retired ICS official, SP Desai, writing in *Hindustan Standard* of December 1944: every day new bamboo sheds and temporary huts are springing up in the reserves. I found that the immigrants absolutely ignore the local officers. The few Nepali graziers and Assamese Pamuas finding no protection from anywhere give *dohai* in the name of the King-Emperor. Verily the cup of humiliation for the Assamese was full.

In a similar manner, the Indira Gandhi government, in collaboration with Assam chief minister Hiteswar Saikia suppressed the people of Assam and their sentiments. They continued to protest and agitate but to no avail. As if to rub salt on their wounds, the central government passed the pernicious Illegal Migrants (Determination by Tribunals) Act in 1983. Hereby, in Assam the onus of proving that a particular person is an infiltrator rested with his complainant or the government of Assam, not on the suspect. The suspect does not have to prove that he is *not a foreigner*. The Foreigners Act of 1946, whereby the onus of proving his bonafides is on the suspect, continues to apply to all other States in India. The only exception made was Assam to help out the illegal migrants.

When travelling from Guwahati to Shillong, one does not spontaneously realise when one has crossed from Assam to Meghalaya. In Meghalaya, the central law was the old 1946 Act! Such has been the discrimination against the Assamese people.

Soon after becoming prime minister in 1985, Rajiv Gandhi ceased to ignore the lamentations of the people of Assam and initiated negotiations, especially with the youth. After much talk, give and take by the stakeholders, an accord was signed. One of its most important clauses was the compiling of a National Register of Citizens. The intention was probably national and not to confine the compilation to Assam, although this State was the priority. But the compilation of this list did not begin for following 30 years until the present ministry at Dispur began the exercise. Incidentally, nothing was done to withdraw the 1983 IMDT Act until the Supreme Court struck it down as ultra vires in 2005.

Having given away one-third of India to Pakistan, paradoxically, Muslims are still pouring into India. This time from Myanmar and Bangladesh (old East Bengal), India's eastern neighbours, just as it did before Partition and after.

ONE EXPLANATION OF INDIA'S BACKWARDNESS

A DISTINGUISHED economist has commented on how ironic it was that the first Green Revolution did not start where it was obviously expected to, from the Doab to the Brahmaputra, ie. from UP to Assam. This was the obvious big belt where it should have flourished, with all its rivers and tributaries and its very fertile soil. It was a ready paradise for an agricultural revolution. Instead, the honour went to Punjab and Haryana. This ignited the writer's curiosity to find out what could have been the reason behind this paradox.

Sir Syed Ahmad Khan, famous in history for being the founder of the Aligarh Muslim University (AMU), was the first Muslim leader of modern India. He was one of the few Muslims in Uttar Pradesh (UP) who was on the side of the British during the Mutiny of 1857, and thus came to wield considerable influence with the rulers. Sir Syed was a member of the Viceroy's Executive Council. He was also the first to declare in 1887 that Hindus and Muslims were separate nations. His co-religionists, he said, were smaller in number, and therefore, had to have reservation in government services as well as in electoral bodies that might come up. Syed's exhortations were further encouragement to the community to continue to adhere to the Islamic ethos which in essence is non-commercial and not greatly concerned about any production. It prefers living off nature's bounty, including womenfolk.

The ethos does not lay much store by way of saving or capital accumulation. Muslims look to Allah to look after them in their hour of need if and when need be. As it happened, nature's bounty has been generously bestowed upon the Indo-Gangetic plain as well as the land of the Brahmaputra. UP, Bihar, Bengal or Assam – where there are more Muslims than in other parts of divided India. Little wonder that the easygoing economic habit infected non-Muslims too in this entire belt, which is backward and by and large, poorer. Bengal, which was an industrially flourishing place at Independence, gradually became the graveyard of factories. The fate that befell Kanpur, hitherto an industrial town, was also that of the whole belt that stretches from Saharanpur in the west to Kamrup in the east.

Partition was meant to bring to a close the mischief of Sir Syed and his Two-Nation theory. Mohammed Ali Jinnah and at least seven of his League colleagues had demanded an exchange of populations, whereby most Muslims would settle in Pakistan and most non-Muslims would live in Hindustan. Under Jawaharlal Nehru, the Congress and its government obstructed this pragmatic and final solution and instead resumed accommodating the two nations all over again in the post-1947 India. In order to stymie the Patelites or the nationalists in the Congress, Nehru played to the Muslim gallery and pampered its members more than he ever did his own children. If any Hindu politician was loved by Muslims it was Nehru. Sardar Patel described him as the only nationalist Muslim that there was.

Nehru ruled India as an unquestioned *badshah* for 17 long years. It was under his watch that this backward belt from Saharanpur to Kamrup sank deeper into a non-productive culture. It continues to be one of the most backward and poorest region in the country. No one has looked back to ask how the ruling class for seven centuries has become backward and less educated. Nor has anyone pointed a finger at either Sir Syed or at Nehru.

Indeed, it would be no exaggeration to say that the backwardness of the four States of Uttar Pradesh, Bihar, Bengal and Assam is the pernicious legacy of Sir Syed Ahmad Khan and Jawaharlal Nehru, which merits serious historical and sociological analysis.

Even as one would have to travel backwards in history to unearth reasons for the phenomenon outlined above, one would be well served to turn to studies on people's work ethic and their socio-religious outlook and the cultures/ethos spawned by it. Renowned German sociologist and political theorist Professor Max Weber's thesis *The Protestant Ethic* shows a close connection between interest and success in capitalist ventures and religious notions of the people. After detailed study, he had come to the conclusion that Protestants valued savings and their investments in productive channels. Hence countries which were predominantly Protestants were industrially more advanced than others.

UP, Bihar, Bengal and Assam have been ruled by Muslims for centuries and the population of these areas developed a conservative spirit in matters of capital enterprises. Agriculture has been the main source of employment and livelihood. Those who owned land had no interest in improving the productivity. All savings made by the ruling and landowning classes were spent on construction of luxurious houses and on the pursuit of pleasure. The advent of British rule brought about a sea change in the economic situation of these States. The British laid a network of railway lines and irrigation canals, leading to the development of industrial centres like Kanpur in UP, and in and around Calcutta in Bengal. By proximity, Bihar and Assam also got an economic boost. In fact, until the departure of the British in 1947, this region acted as an engine of growth.

With such a promising beginning, it was natural that these States should have galloped ahead in growth in post-1947 India. The fact that they have not, but have instead fallen into the backwaters of development indicates that entrepreneurship is missing. This, in turn, can be traced to the feudal mentality developed during the Muslim era.

The level of per capita income is the widely accepted indicator of economic development. This is further supplemented by data on the share of industry in total Gross Domestic Product (GDP). The progress of the States has also begun to be measured by Human Development Indices. Based on these yardsticks, it is seen that States like Uttar Pradesh, Bihar, West Bengal and Assam stand nowhere in comparison to Maharashtra, Gujarat, Tamil Nadu and Goa. The three tables below provide a brief idea of the relative economic backwardness of the North and North Eastern States.

Table 1: State-wise Human Development Index (HDI) Score and Ranks: 1983 to 2011-12 (Rural & Urban Combined)

State	1983	1987-88	1993	1999-2000	2004-05	2009-10	2011-12
Andhra Pradesh	0.290 (14)	0.185 (16)	0.217 (18)	0.288 (14)	0.298 (16)	0.286 (16)	0.309 (17)
Arunachal Pradesh	0.116 (24)	0.006 (24)	0.110 (22)	0.168 (21)	0.234 (21)	0.175 (23)	0.124 (27)
Assam	0.242 (17)	0.123 (20)	0.147 (21)	0.144 (25)	0.234 (22)	0.176 (22)	0.138 (26)
Bihar	0.071 (27)	0.024 (27)	0.061 (27)	0.074 (28)	0.050 (28)	0.050 (28)	0.158 (25)
Chhattisgarh*	0.129 (22)	0.077 (22)	0.069 (23)	0.155 (23)	0.142 (27)	0.114 (27)	0.180 (24)
Goa	0.774 (2)	0.540 (2)	0.700 (2)	0.701 (2)	0.781 (2)	0.796 (2)	0.803 (2)
Gujrat	0.502 (8)	0.301 (12)	0.362 (10)	0.390 (11)	0.429 (12)	0.461 (8)	0.477 (10)
Haryana	0.556 (5)	0.415 (7)	0.396 (8)	0.490 (7)	0.544 (7)	0.516 (7)	0.493 (7)
Himachal Pradesh	0.622 (4)	0.461 (5)	0.430 (7)	0.550 (5)	0.605 (4)	0.655 (3)	0.647 (3)
Jammu & Kashmir	0.443 (9)	0.289 (3)	0.316 (13)	0.406 (10)	0.493 (9)	0.443 (11)	0.479 (9)
Jharkhand*	0.071 (27)	0.024 (27)	0.061 (27)	0.077 (27)	0.145 (26)	0.160 (26)	0.222 (21)
Karnataka	0.416 (10)	0.342 (10)	0.326 (12)	0.379 (12)	0.436 (11)	0.457 (9)	0.420 (12)
Kerala	0.818 (1)	0.722 (1)	0.805 (1)	0.815 (1)	1.000 (1)	0.963 (1)	0.9141 (1)
Madhya Pradesh	0.129 (22)	0.077 (22)	0.069 (23)	0.152 (24)	0.182 (23)	0.172 (24)	0.186 (23)
Maharashtra	0.504 (7)	0.408 (8)	0.446 (5)	0.506 (6)	0.583 (6)	0.602 (5)	0.629 (5)
Manipur	0.305 (13)	0.205 (14)	0.259 (15)	0.271 (16)	0.256 (19)	0.217 (21)	0.199 (22)
Meghalaya	0.215 (18)	0.124 (19)	0.225 (16)	0.260 (18)	0.340 (14)	0.259 (18)	0.246 (20)

Mizoram	0.547 (6)	0.449 (6)	0.613 (3)	0.576 (4)	0.529 (8)	0.449 (10)	0.408 (13)
Nagaland	0.272 (15)	0.476 (4)	0.438 (6)	0.467 (8)	0.403 (13)	0.262 (17)	0.257 (19)
Odisha	0.187 (20)	0.141 (18)	0.159 (19)	0.175 (20)	0.174 (24)	0.248 (19)	0.261 (18)
Punjab	0.691 (3)	0.519 (3)	0.562 (4)	0.578 (3)	0.640 (3)	0.584 (6)	0.538 (6)
Rajasthan	0.181 (21)	0.081 (21)	0.155 (20)	0.265 (17)	0.278 (18)	0.240 (20)	0.324 (16)
Sikkim	0.211 (19)	0.160 (17)	0.217 (17)	0.236 (19)	0.299 (15)	0.377 (15)	0.324 (15)
Tamil Nadu	0.359 (11)	0.345 (9)	0.387 (9)	0.462 (9)	0.587 (5)	0.621 (4)	0.633 (4)
Tripura	0.258 (16)	0.205 (15)	0.280 (14)	0.285 (15)	0.288 (17)	0.421 (12)	0.354 (14)
Uttar Pradesh	0.102 (25)	0.058 (25)	0.066 (25)	0.142 (26)	0.167 (25)	0.168 (25)	0.122 (28)
Uttarakhand*	0.102 (25)	0.058 (25)	0.066 (25)	0.162 (22)	0.247 (20)	0.378 (14)	0.426 (11)
West Bengal	0.324 (12)	0.318 (11)	0.353 (11)	0.371 (13)	0.462 (10)	0.409 (13)	0.483 (8)

Note: Figure in the parenthesis show the ranks

*Prior to 2004-05, HDI score and rank is same as the mother State.

Source: Constructed by author

Table 2: State-wise Per Capita Income (2011-2012, in Rs)

Assam	33,633
Bihar	24,681
Tamil Nadu	84,058
Uttar Pradesh	29,417
West Bengal	55,864
Maharashtra	83,471
Gujarat	75,115
Goa	1,92,652

Table 3: State-wise Gross State Domestic Product (GDP) by Industry of Origin (at 2004-2005 prices, Rs in crores)

For year 2013-14

	Agriculture and Allied	Industry	Total
Assam	18829	18829	88537
Bihar	33015	32106	174734
Uttar Pradesh	103378	98724	465969
W.Bengal	62236	68798	374899
Maharashtra	67673	255243	89778
Gujarat	47594	167325	427219
Goa	986	9530	28255
Tamil Nadu	34988	139469	480618

(*Source*: CSO, Govt. of India)

The story of Indian regions that were once under Islamic rule is no different from that of Islamic countries in the Middle East. It would be instructive for us to look at how Islamic law held back the Middle East as well.

Professor Timur Kuran, Professor of Islamic Studies at Duke University in his book, *The Long Divergence: How Islamic Law Held Back the Middle East,* has pointed to certain shortcomings in Islamic law that are responsible for the Middle East being not able to keep pace with the industrialisation of the Western countries. In particular, he has referred to the Islamic law of commercial partnerships; its inheritance system; the religious endowments system and individualism of Islamic law. During the first millennium, during pre-Islamic times and the early years of Islam, the Middle East was much ahead of countries in Western Europe. However, it suffered a decline in the second millennium for reasons mentioned above.

Institutions are systems of socially produced regularities that shape and, are in turn, shaped by individual behaviour. An institution of great importance to Middle Eastern daily life was the holy law of Islam, *Sharia*, (Islamic law). In principle, Islamic law covered all human activity. In the political discourse of the Ottoman Empire (1299 AD-1922 AD) there was even a category of laws known as 'ruler's law' (*kanun*), as distinct from Islamic law, and also a third category, customary law (*orf*), which rested on precedent rather than religious scripture or learning.

The two areas in which the Middle East fell conspicuously behind, right up to modem times were: People entered into contracts that followed an Islamic template, enforced through Islamic courts. They apportioned estates according to Islamic inheritance rules. Residents of the region's cities obtained services mostly from *wakfs*, which were trusts formed under Islamic law and supervised by officials with religious training. Almost all law suits involving at least one Muslim were litigated by Muslim judges, under Islamic legal principles. Cracking this puzzle thus requires close attention to the practical consequences of Islamic law. With respect to economic institutions, the 8th and 9th centuries saw the emergence of an Islamic law to govern the trusts known as wakfs as well as the refinement of the Islamic law of partnership. Successful imitation of foreigners required the transplantation of alien institutions, such as stock markets, municipalities, and laws supportive of large companies capable of outliving their founders.

Commercial partnerships formed under Islamic law typically involved a few partners who pooled resources for short-lived ventures, whereas Westerners were forming indefinitely lasting enterprises with tens, hundreds, and even thousands of shareholders. In traditional Middle Eastern credit markets, suppliers typically were individuals capable of giving small loans. Westerners had access to commercial banks that could channel capital mobilised from the masses into large-scale productive ventures. No stock markets existed for trading shares of indigenous Middle Eastern companies, which tended to be ephemeral. Stock markets were gaining prominence in the West, where investors in long-living enterprises liquidated shares at will.

The supply of urban social services is another area of contrast. In the Middle East, the traditional provider was the wakf. In the face of breathtaking technological advances, this form of trust proved inadequate as a vehicle for keeping services up to date. The municipality, a standard instrument of local governance in Western Europe, was better suited to the rapidly changing needs of cities. Institutions borrowed from the West were used also to limit Western influences, preserve old customs, and even invent new traditions.

The term Islamic bank or banking is heard a lot these days. From a historical perspective the concept of an 'Islamic bank' is a contradiction in terms. An Islamic bank operates on a scale far larger than any private enterprise the Middle East knew before the 19th century. It is a corporation, an organisation alien to Islamic law. Islamic banking thus constitutes an 'invented tradition'. Its architects have used Western institutional models not to make Muslim economic life more Western but, rather, to encourage saving, investing, borrowing, and lending in ways at least cosmetically Islamic. Their shared goal was to replicate specific Western achievements, not to appropriate Western culture indiscriminately.

By the mid-19th century, which marks the initiation of major reforms, the world had entered a new economic epoch, that of modern economic growth. Its chief characteristic is itself-sustaining economic expansion at an unprecedented rate; although contractions can occur, they amount to temporary reversals along an upward path. If this is granted, it is simply a matter of record that until well after 1750 AD, considered the start of modern economic growth, the Middle East lacked the organisational forms and techniques.

The first Arab Human Development Report, issued in 2002 by a commission composed entirely of Arab thinkers, points to a 'freedom deficit' and a 'human capabilities/knowledge deficit' as two characteristics of the Arab world today. The former deficit refers mainly to governance patterns inimical to civil and political freedom and the latter to low educational attainment, access to information, and intellectual creativity. At the beginning of the new millennium, the Middle East had become a technological slow coach; its states discouraged investment, its inhabitants were poorly educated, and its intellectual life lacked vigour and it had made little advance from the 19th century.

In the 19th century, the Middle East was a laggard on both counts. It lacked the know-how essential for mass production as surely as it lacked a law of corporations. England, Germany, and France had both, which enabled their entrepreneurs to form huge companies capable of exploiting new technologies.

Hence, Middle Eastern entrepreneurs had trouble competing in the global economy because of both technological and organisational stagnation. The absence of markets for trading company shares posed a more intractable obstacle to the Middle East's economic advancement than its delays in mechanising.

Institutions of governance are no easier to transplant than those of commerce or civil society. Witness the Arab Middle East's persistently low international rankings relating to civil rights, government effectiveness, and rule of law, in spite of political reforms over the past century (table 4).

Table 4: Comparative Indicators of Political Performance (2008-2009)

Region, country, or grouping	Civil liberties 1 (most) to 10	Political rights 1 (strongest) to 10	Corruption perceptions 1 to 10 (least corrupt)	Rule of law (-) -2.5 to 2.5 (best)
Middle East	5.1	5.6	2.9	-0.3
Arab League	5.4	6.2	2.8	-0.6
Iran	6.0	6.0	1.8	-0.8
Turkey	3.0	3.0	4.0	0.1
OECD (except Turkey)	1.4	1.1	6.8	1.2
China	6.0	7.0	3.6	-0.3

It is in turning our gaze to segments of the social system beyond direct state control that stagnant practices become salient. Insofar as inertia explains the Middle East's failure to keep up with Western Europe, it is private economic life, not public administration, which calls for primary attention. To put it in terms of the tripartite legal categorisation familiar to historians, religious law and customary law merit analytic priority over ruler's law.

In discourses on why the Middle East became underdeveloped, a commonly articulated explanation points the finger at outsiders. The machinations of Europeans, the author says, turned the region into a 'dependent', 'plundered' and 'self-doubting' part of the world. But such interpretations that attribute the region's underdevelopment to foreign meddling miss vital ingredients of the historical record. Understanding the factors responsible for the West's dynamism will help to isolate obstacles to self-generated development in the Middle East. They will elucidate also why Islamic institutions well adapted to medieval conditions seemed impoverished a millennium later. The purpose is to examine the dynamics of private economic organisation in the pre-modern Middle East. Why critical transformations failed to occur is the question one must answer. Where the particulars involve religion, it is to religion that the argument must lead.

The Islamic inheritance system spread wealth by providing mandatory inheritance shares to all sons and daughters, and Islamic polygamy had the same effect by enabling the wealthiest merchants to have unusually numerous heirs. What could scarcely have been understood in the early Islamic centuries is that in the face of outside developments, these institutions would eventually incapacitate Muslim merchants in their dealings with the West, in world markets, and even at partnership.

Over time, the curriculum changed less in *madrasas* as compared to universities, contributing greatly to the Middle East becoming an intellectual backwater, though in the 9th and 10th centuries it provided some of the brightest concepts to the world. Although many factors contributed to the region's lack of intellectual prominence after several bright centuries under Islamic rule, a basic cause lies in the wakfs' organisational limitations. Madrasas and universities were both non-profit organisations.

The wakf became Islam's main organisational form for providing social services at a time when Western Europe deployed the corporation for many of the other ends. The organisational gap widened in the late 16th century, when the West began applying the corporate form of organisation to profit-oriented production, finance and commerce. For example, the universities of Paris and Oxford, initially set up as trusts in the 12th and 13th centuries, had become self-governing and self-renewing in due course.

Islam's relatively egalitarian inheritance system raised the costs of liquidating a partnership prematurely, thereby limiting the size and duration of partnerships, fragmenting the estates of successful merchants, and hindering the preservation of businesses across generations. The dynamic consequences are critical here. Members of small and short-lived partnerships felt no urge to develop sophisticated accounting methods or to obtain greater liquidity through tradability. An unintended consequence of such stagnation is that the business community could not even contemplate using an organisational form akin to the corporation.

If the structural stagnation of commercial partnerships constituted one reason for the dearth of organisational innovation in general, another was that successful merchants tended to convert their wealth into real estate, for reconversion into the corpus of a wakf. They did so for the very reason why founding wakfs gained enormous popularity among high officials: the weakness of private property rights. Like other wealthy groups, prosperous merchants sheltered wealth within wakfs.

Why did the Middle East enter the 19th century as an underdeveloped region? The critical deficiencies were frozen wakf assets, atomistic financial markets, courts unsuited to impersonal exchange – none comprehended how such features were mutually reinforcing, or how they were blocking transformations essential to global competitiveness.

Through wakfs, residents benefited from subsidised social services. Economic disputes were settled informally through arbitration or formally through courts that rendered judgments quickly. Islamic law was not considered harmful to economic progress. By the same token, the reasons why the Middle East fell behind would have remained a mystery. To explain the lack of the region's modernisation, and Islam's role in it, we have to focus on aspects of the Middle East's organisational heritage that turned into weaknesses gradually, through transformations elsewhere.

An Islamic partnership lacked entity shielding, in that any member could force its dissolution unilaterally, and its assets were exposed to demands from third parties. The death of partner terminated the partnership automatically, giving his heirs an immediate claim on a share of the assets; all surviving members incurred costs. The number of heirs could be large, because Islam's inheritance law assigns mandatory shares to designated relatives of the descendant. The partnership termination rule, like the lack of entity shielding, thus discouraged the formation of large and long-lived partnerships. Merchants and investors would form small and short-lived partnerships in order to lessen the risks of untimely dissolution. In allowing polygamy, Islam compounded the incentives to keep partnerships atomistic and ephemeral. This is because merchants with multiple wives tended to have more heirs. Rarely did the business empires of the most successful merchants survive them, because their estates got divided into too many pieces to make recombination practical. Incentives to trade share were dampened. In sum, several self-enforcing elements of Islamic law-contracting provisions, inheritance system and marriage regulations jointly contributed to the stagnation of the Middle East's commercial infrastructure (table 5).

Table 5: Islamic Institutions that Helped to Delay Economic Modernisation

Present in Islam's first few decades	Developed in mostly or entirely Islam's initial period
Inheritance system	Contact law
Acceptance of polygamy	Waqf
Ban of *riba*	Court system
Absence of corporation	Capitulations
Choice of law limited to non-Muslims	
Prohibition of apostasy	
Absence of merchant organisations	

The Islamic inheritance system delayed organisational modernisation only because, with the corporation precluded, the partnership remained the only possible starting point for developing durable and large commercial organisations.

The third of the seven problematic institutions present

from the beginning, the ban on *riba*, interest, was a steady irritant to suppliers and users of credit. By requiring the use of stratagems, it raised credit costs. Although Islamic banks ostensibly do only interest-free business, in reality they give and take interest through means resembling the stratagems used in medieval financial markets.

The emergence of the Islamic legal system without a concept of corporation contributed to keeping Middle Eastern businesses atomistic. The final problematic pattern that was present at the birth of Islam is the absence of merchant organisations serving them in foreign lands.

The fifth original institution was the choice of law. Allowing Islamic law to trump the legal systems of non-Muslims, and permitting anyone to sue in Islamic court at will, depressed the competition faced by Islamic courts.

Both the Quran and the remembered sayings of Prophet Muhammad contain references to apostasy as a religious offense. On the basis of these references, Muslim jurists of the 7th century declared apostasy punishable by death. The severity of this punishment doubtless contributed to the outcomes of Islamic legal pluralism.

Thus, Islamic inheritance system and its marriage regulations jointly hindered indigenous organisational modernisation. It was only when modern organisations were transplanted from abroad that they ceased to harm economic performance in the Middle East.

The same is true of the Muslim populations in the Indo-Gangetic plains, ie. in the States where such populations are in considerable number. Though cities like Calcutta and Kanpur were India's first industrial growth hubs, slowly, these centres and their economies disintegrated and despite the land's fertility, economic growth became a dream. Paradoxically, India's most fertile land became the most backward.

WHAT IMRAN KHAN FORGOT

PRIME MINISTER Imran Khan of Pakistan has offered to teach India how to treat its minorities. Is it not likely that when he said this, he was experiencing a flashback to his cricketing days, when our fast bowlers were not comparable to his country's pace attack? Traditionally, in the undivided India, it was the Punjab that produced pacemen. The one outstanding name that comes to the writer's mind is that of Mohammad Nissar, the fastest opening bowler the subcontinent had produced in his day. Certainly, even now, their pack of speed merchants may have something to teach our players.

An Oxonian had once said: Imran is cricket and cricket is Imran. Similarly, Zubin Mehta is music and cannot be imagined in terms of cricket. So also, it is difficult to reconcile the Imran image with prime ministership. It is not impossible that while he was talking of minorities, his mind was on how to teach India to play cricket and to play in India at the Eden Gardens.

It goes without saying that he has not seen the holocaust of Hindus and Sikhs starting with Rawalpindi in 1947, nor does he know how his Christian compatriots had rejoiced at the birth of Pakistan only to subsequently regret it, plus of course, being frequently accused of blasphemy. The Communist Party had wholeheartedly sponsored Partition, only to later beat its breast – it was simply eliminated by the torrent of Islam.

The Ahmediyas, whose hero Sir Mohammad Zafarullah Khan had drafted the Pakistan Resolution of March 1940, also had their taste of the 'glory' of the state they helped give birth to. Imran Khan was certainly not born then to witness the magnificent work done by Sir Zafarullah. Nor perhaps in 1953, when the latter's house in Lahore was set on fire, which induced him to flee Pakistan and not return until his dying days. The rest of his years he spent at The Hague in the Netherlands to bring majesty to the glittering benches of the International Court of Justice. In the meantime, the charismatic Prime Minister Zulfikar Ali Bhutto expelled the Ahmediyas from the sanctified garden of Islam.

Another Ahmediya hero who brought glory to Imran's country was Dr Abdul Qadeer Khan, whose thuggish doings in the Netherlands enabled him to obtain the secrets of the atomic bomb, all, of course, in the cause of Khidmat-e-Allah, the first Islamic nuclear bomb. He, too, was rewarded by his faith by being expelled.

This writer was educated by two men. The first was his grandfather, one of whose friends was Ahmed Ali Jinnah. He relished Parsi humour and claimed to be culturally a Parsi. Although he was not a practicing Muslim, he acquainted grandfather with his insights into Islam. That, when a Muslim wishes to convert someone, it is with the best intention of opening a possible chance of the convert entering *jannat.* No other god can enable a non-believer to cross the gateway of heaven.

The second gentleman who taught this writer was his spoken Urdu teacher, who did not overtly suggest a conversion but did say that the future lay with Islam. Just extrapolate the progress of a number of religions. The Yehudis (Jews) have reduced in number and shrunk to a fraction of what they were. The Christians have scattered into many denominations. Many a worshipper in Europe has given up worship. Christianity's priests have come to Asia, where according to the late Pope John Paul II, there are innumerable souls to harvest. Contrast these performances with the progress of Islam, whose tide is continually rising.

It is ironical that Prime Minister Imran Khan should want to teach India how to treat its minorities. He has held out Pakistan as an example of good treatment. He is probably unaware that Rafiq Zakaria, in his widely read book, *The Man who Divided India*, has clearly stated that but for the Muslims of UP (especially Aligarh), Bihar and Bombay, Pakistan might not have been. Young men from Aligarh went all the way to Punjab to campaign for the 1945-46 general elections, which proved decisive for Partition. They propagated Pakistan as the new Medina.

Imran should note, if India should seriously follow the Pakistani example, it should reduce its minority population as Pakistan did to three per cent from the 22 in 1947. Does the cricketing legend expect his country, with its vast land space, to absorb up to 201 million Muslims now in India? He could not have forgotten his cricket and probably believes that greater the population, the higher are the chances of throwing up more players. If not, the new Prime Minister has forgotten that his country has created a new minority with the passing of every decade.

The saga of creating ever new minorities began with the Sikhs at Rawalpindi; soon thereafter, the Hindus. Then came the turn of the Ahmediyas at Lahore. Pakistan's Christians who had backed Partition, in due course, became unpopular enough to be frequently accused of blasphemy and awarded the death sentence by being stoned. The Baloch, of course, were never fully trusted but gradually became suspected if not also positively distrusted. The latest is the turn of the Shias, who are routinely killed by bombs while praying. There is also a proposal to expel Shias from the fraternity of Islam. They are followers of Imam Hussein, who was the grandson of Prophet Muhammad. A distinguished Shia was Qaid-e-Azam Jinnah without whom Pakistan might not have been.

Ever since his college days, this writer has been told that all Sunni Muslims of the world belong to a single community, which is their first loyalty. It is, therefore, a mystery why most Pakistanis are callous about the safety, security and welfare of their brethren in India? Islamabad's regimes pursue their own interests without caring for any repercussion on Muslims in India. Earlier, their great guru was the USA. Now, they look to China for direction; ostensibly, others be damned. This is as old a syndrome as in 1947. Within two months, Pakistan had no compunction in invading the Kashmir Valley.

As long ago as 1951, Zakir Husain, then Vice-Chancellor of the Aligarh Muslim University and later President, took the lead along with 13 other Muslims eminences to submit a memorandum to Frank P Graham, the United Nations representative in Kashmir, on 14 August 1951 which said:

> Is indeed a pity that India has never thought of taking the help of its Muslim citizens, most of whom can be the country's useful allies against Pakistani misdemeanour. There is no doubt a problem. About the only viable Muslim leadership in the country is ecclesiastical. The luminaries, who are not *maulvis*, do not have sufficient following. Addressing Muslim citizens through the *ulema* has its limitations. The substantive interest of the masses lies in a peaceful life where the individual and his family can try and prosper, to educate the children and so on. Whereas the thrust of the *ulema* would be to protect and promote the influence of Islam. The leaders of India, therefore, should find a channel of informing and seeking cooperation of our Muslim brethren directly.

The memorandum was also signed by Sir Sultan Ahmed, Sir Mohammed Usman, both former members of the Viceroy's Council. The signatories included the Nawab of Chhatari, Chief Justice of Allahabad, Sir Iqbal Ahmed, Sir Fazal Rahimtoola, AK Khwaja, TM Zarif, BH Zaidi and Hafi-ur-Rehman; the last two were MPs. Their submission also said:

> If the Hindus are not welcome in Pakistan, how can we, in all fairness, expect Muslims to be welcomed in India? Such a policy must inevitably, as the past has already shown, result in the uprooting of Muslims in this country and their migration

> to Pakistan, where as it became clear last year, they are no longer welcome, lest their influx should destroy Pakistan's economy.

There was also a background to this fear. Several Muslim League leaders had repeatedly emphasised in the years preceding Partition that when the country was divided, there must be an exchange of population. Sir Feroze Khan Noon had gone to the extent of threatening the re-enactment of the violent orgies of Chengiz Khan and Halaqu Khan. Paradoxically, there was no population exchange in 1947 when the country was divided, Muslims continue to live peacefully in India. Imran Khan should remember, thankfully, India does not treat its minorities as Pakistan has done for the last 70 years and if Pakistan is home to 203 million Muslims, India is home to 201 million Muslims. And, India is not sendig them all to Pakistan yet.

CHARACTER OVER ABILITY

EDUCATION IS WEALTH

IN 1925, MY aunt Saraswati Vora stood 33rd in the Bombay Presidency matriculation. The marks scored by her were the highest amongst the comparatively few girls who appeared. The occasion was therefore celebrated as special by our community, especially by the womenfolk. We can imagine what a small proportion of people studied as far as matriculation, especially so from among the *bania* community. It largely considered studies beyond the three Rs to be a waste of time and which delayed the boys' entry into business. Some families went to the extent of considering higher education to be a handicap in the conduct of commerce. The more one has studied, the greater is the likelihood of the person seeing too many angles to a proposition and becoming indecisive!

Today, education is seen as wealth. In his latest book entitled *The New Wealth of Nations*, Surjit S Bhalla describes the 'acquisition of education as the acquisition of wealth'. Less than 250 years ago, Adam Smith wrote *The Wealth of Nations* in which he expounded that the 'invisible hand of competition' guided an economic system based on individual self-interest.

Why go that far? When I began working, I was told by some business captains that the key to wealth is *instinct,* if not also an *intuition,* for finance is the key to creating wealth. With the advent and growth of Information Technology, however, knowledge began becoming the key to wealth. That is when the balance of big business started tilting to south India whether in Bengaluru, Hyderabad or Chennai from Mumbai and to an extent, to Kolkata.

Bhalla has a wide vision of education as wealth. It also makes individuals in a society more equal; women get empowered and become equal to men. Similarly, countries, because of their educated citizens, become more equal. To remain wealthy with the help of property has become difficult after the abolition of the princely States, of *jagirdar*is and *zamindar*is, as well as due to the land reforms which took place over the years after Independence. Mega-industrialists are a small percentage of the population. As a result, to become a Bill Gates or Jeff Bezos, the promoter of Amazon, the e-commerce king, it is education reinforced by imagination that is needed.

The Government of Delhi deserves to be generously complimented for realising the importance of schooling, and that also under the State umbrella. Not many families can afford to pay the fees of unaided schools and, like anywhere else in the world including the USA, the State has to take the brunt of the responsibility. For the quality and kind of teaching to come up across the country in State schools would take time to materialise and be equal to the challenge. A primary reason for parents preferring private or unaided schools is the medium of instruction. Without knowing how to speak and write simple English, it is difficult to get a reasonably well-paying job. It has always been so in our country since the advent of the British in India.

The realisation that the question affected the masses as much dawned when the youth of class 3 and 4 families began aspiring for well-paid employment. This need has been becoming obvious over the last 30 years. Many a school across the country has switched to English medium, partly or entirely. Those that have not changed have lost students or even closed down. The changeover in Delhi has begun only lately though, and for it to now take place quickly is not possible because teachers in English are comparatively few. Hence Hindi will have to remain the main name of the game.

The unaided schools are about a third of the total schools in Delhi, if we bear in mind that the municipalities too run primary classes. They would have to be depended upon until the State institutions are fully upgraded in every way. A sufficient number of teachers who can teach well in English have to be developed. Until then, care should be taken to protect and nurture the English medium schools that the country has, whichever sector they be, State, aided or unaided. With the advent of the Right to Education Act, 2009, unaided schools are under severe pressure, which is not widely realised. The reason is that 25 per cent of the students have to be taught free as they are economically weaker. That means that the schools' expenditure has to be met from the fees collected from only

75 per cent of the pupils. 'Charge 75 but teach 100' is the economic theme song.

For the Union Territories including Delhi, the staff and teachers have to be paid on the basis of the 7th Pay Commission. If the fees are commensurately raised, many parents can pay but some find it difficult and protest. The one solution to this knotty problem would be for the governments to give the parents, truly under pressure, a limited scholarship per student. If that is not possible, let the private schools increase fees to the extent justified by the increase in expenditure. It is not in the national interest to squeeze the schools for the sake of only a percentage of their students. Instead, the schools should be induced, encouraged and helped to expand in order to teach more children. To strangulate them would be to gradually destroy them without developing their competent alternatives in the State sector.

When I was at schooling age, Kolkata's best institutions were the Hare School and the Ballygunge Government School. They were owned and run by the Bengal State and were preferred even by the wealthiest of parents. Their children were sent to the famous missionary institutes only if they failed to get admission to Hare or Ballygunge. To build up schools of such excellence on a large scale would take time. Until then, we must avoid socialism for the sake of some. After all, the Soviet system as well as its ideology was destroyed by its own self.

Not only the pupils but also a few parents need to be explained, if not also educated. Well-known schools do not have to seek out applicants. In Delhi, they apply spontaneously, and their children join if they are lucky. After two or three years, a few parents begin nit-picking and gradually become grievance treasuries until they end up complaining to the government. If they happen to have a contact or two, the authorities lend an ear and a ding-dong begins. The bigger schools have thousands of students to teach and attend to their problems, apart from administrative duties and answering to occasional emergencies. The question is: how much teacher energy should be devoted to the thousands of youngsters and how much to the odd nitpickers?

There are others who relish litigation and petition the honourable High Court, which has little choice but to hear both sides and eventually issue an order. There is a separate tribunal where teachers and staff members can petition for the wrongs done to them. But there is no tribunal for dealing with parent grievances. In the bargain, the community of schools has to knock the High Court doors more often than corporate houses! The paradox is… good schools and good teachers are rare, so are responsible parents in a nation of one billion plus.

THE BANIAS

NEAR THE share broker office of Messrs Kishanchand Jhunjhunwala in Lyons Range of Calcutta, I was introduced to a Comrade Biyani. He was an unusual *bania*. For, on the one hand, he dealt in shares and, on the other, he was a communist. He claimed to be a member of the Communist Party of India (CPI) and appeared to speak about Leftism with conviction. In the half an hour or so that I heard him, he said that Peking (now Beijing) was not happy with New Delhi's attitude on the Sino-Indian border; something I had no idea about at the time. He was primarily addressing our common friend who had incidentally introduced me, and I was listening in. He also said that before long the Sino-Soviet differences would begin to come into the open. Again, to my 19-year-old mind, it was startling news; if I remember right it must have been the November of 1956.

The chitchat soon shifted to the share market and some

controversy over some share scrips pledged to his creditor by the much-talked about takeover magnet Haridas Mundhra. The meteor was glowing, and my friend happened to say that everything would be sorted out amicably. This complacence had a provocative effect on Biyani who exclaimed that my friend did not know what a real bania was like. You Gujaratis are at best second class banias, he asserted. He knew of a young businessman who had settled in Bombay and lived in a posh multi-storeyed building. While he was away on a business tour, his wife got involved with a neighbour and several other neighbours came to know about it. She was naturally embarrassed as well as nervous about her husband's retribution. After a day or two of cool thinking, she had decided her tactic.

As soon as he returned home, she began bombarding him with her woes. Why should he stay away from Bombay so often and for so long, leaving her unprotected from lecherous neighbours? How she had been molested by the rascal so-and-so. How traumatised she was. What a terrible humiliation it was for a respectable young woman. The wife went on in this wailing vein for a good half an hour. The husband listened to her patiently until she stopped for a breath or two. When she did, he consoled her saying not to worry. These things happen. It could have happened even if he was in Bombay but away at office and so on. And then, he went on to deliver his punch line. He declared, 'after all darling, the lecherous neighbour gave you something. He didn't take anything away'.

Such is the soul of the bania. 'Material gain is the single greatest driving force' said the proletarian friend, condemning the Indian bourgeoisie. If sin is committed in the pursuit of gain, the mocking tone continued, 'it is washed away by the daily Ganesh puja and the periodical pilgrimage to Tirupati, Varanasi or wherever'. Many years later when I happened to narrate this conversation to my friend Indrajit Thakkar in Bombay, he was reminded of what the *Times*, London, had said about the British Prime Minister Lord Attlee on his death. That he was a politician without a lust for power, rather like a lover without passion. Craving is an undoubted ingredient of success and the bania who gets rich usually has a craving for wealth.

All *vaishya*s are banias but the ones from Rajasthan are exceptional. They are known as Marwaris although only those from Marwar or the Jodhpur area should strictly speaking be called so. But the non-vaishyas are not called Marwaris. They are known as Rajputs, Jats, Muslims and so on. On the other hand, the vaishyas from Shekhawati (Jaipur), Mewar (Udaipur) etc. are all happy to be referred to as Marwaris.

I grew up with the impression that Marwaris are stingy because whenever my mother or her siblings wanted to accuse anyone of being miserly, they called him a Marwari. But there was no contact with any person of the community nor any discussion that I could remember. My father worked for Birla Brothers since 1944. Although he was well looked after, he did feel that the Birlas favoured Marwari managers. It did not really concern me until 1952 when my parents had taken me to Bombay to put me in college.

Just about the time during June, there had been a mini-crash in the Bombay share market and the focus was on an operator named Bajarang Birla. He had defaulted on his commitments and was a particular object of bitterness because he was mistaken to be a proxy for a large house. He offered to settle his debts for four annas which meant pay up 25 paise for every rupee he owed provided there would be no future claim on the same transaction. Among the Gujaratis (including Parsi) circle, there was a great deal of loose criticism about the Marwaris. How could a whole community be answerable for the default by one? Whenever my father tried to argue, his acquaintances accused him of having sold himself to his employers.

I soon got busy in Elphinstone College and hardly came across anyone who was identified as a Marwari. Ashok Birla, son of Gajanan and grandson of Rameshwar Das Birla, elder brother of the great GD, joined my college in 1955. I never met him, but I do remember he was soon fined Rs 40. For a few days, he was the talk of the college because none had ever before been fined more than Rs 20 at Elphinstone. Or so was the popular impression. This was the same Ashok Birla who unfortunately died in the Airbus 320 crash at Bangalore in 1990.

Soon after graduating in 1956, I was quite happy to join Birla Brothers if only my father would introduce me to the organisation. As I had described at length in a letter on the Birla Brothers to my colleague SP Roy, Maganlal Gandhi, the chief executive of Century Mills and a distant relative of mine, recommended them as employers who offered a scope for rapid success.

About this time, two acquaintances of my father's from Saurashtra happened to visit Calcutta. They had some work with several companies including a Birla firm. They sought an introduction from my father but, at the same time, kept running down Marwaris as people who reveled in black money, people who were the Jews of India and so on. I had read a bit about the Nazis and the Jews. Somehow, the comparison was unconvincing; the Jewish cap did not fit the Marwari. But I kept a reflection on the subject pending until I got an opportunity to interact with some more Jews. In college, I had an acquaintance called Abraham Benjamin who was the nicest of chaps. In the National Cadet Corps, I had a co-cadet called Mordecai who was also pleasant. For all that Adolf Hitler had done to the community, I had only sympathy for it.

My own interaction with Marwari individuals began after I joined J. Thomas & Co., a firm of brokers, in 1957. The company's gunny (jute fabric) department had a family called Almal as banias who underwrote any loss that might occur as a result of default by an Indian client. Most British firms had such a system of safety because the expatriates could not know Indian traders sufficiently. There was Sagarmal, the elder brother, Ram Narain the younger, whose son in turn was Satya Narain. I was the first Indian covenanted assistant or executive that this department had ever appointed. Otherwise, it had been a den of Scots.

The Almals were cool towards me. They did not help me in my attempts to learn the trade and get on. They would veto any transactions that I worked out with Indian parties. Being underwriters, they had a veto power over all contracts that needed a guarantee. Even small, short or near-term business with houses like the Ispahanis, they would reject. I was only 21 then and could not understand why. As it happened, the company decided to close down its gunny department in February 1959 or 14 months after my joining as it was making losses. Before

I went off on transfer to the tea department, I said goodbye to them. Sagarmal was inarticulate. Satya Narain looked sad but his father Ram Narain implicitly apologised for appearing to be non-cooperative all these months. In his 40 years, he had not seen a Scot really understanding the speculative, fluctuating gunny market in less than five years, whereas I had got going in five weeks. To them, I seemed a miracle if not also a threat to their position. He had not realised that I had some exposure to forward trading due to my casual stint at the share market. Anyway, he wished me well and expressed his regret at my leaving gunnies so dear to him and his family for nearly a century. The Almal candour indeed touched me.

While on the subject of forward trading, at the share market I had had occasion to hear Chiranjeevlal Jhunjhunwala, son of the Kishanchand I mentioned earlier. He had explained to me the Marwari theory of how to speculate. It contrasted sharply with what Messrs Nanji Shyamji, a Gujarati firm of gunny exporters, did in 1958. They had expected large-scale buying of gunny bags by China. In anticipation, they had built up a big long position in the forward market. In other words, hook line and sinker they were bullish and bought a large quantity. They had bought B Twills, a standard variety dealt on the forward market, upto Rs121 for 100 bags.

PJP Thomas, the London principal of J. Thomas & Co. was visiting Calcutta and all the covenanted executives were invited for lunch to meet him. It was a cool bright December morning. B Twills were trading at Rs116 when my colleagues and I left the office for the venue of the lunch a little before one o'clock. We returned by 2.30 pm to learn that B Twills had crashed to Rs 87, all in a matter of two hours. We were told that Nanji Shamji had failed and defaulted on payments in the forward market. I did not know, although the more experienced people must have been aware that the firm had continued to buy despite negative signals from China. The Sino-Indian border had already become a source of tension and the government agency in Peking would rather not buy Indian goods. Nanji Shyamji kept averaging their losses in the hope that something would happen whereupon prices would flare up and they could get out of their commitment without a loss. They had hoped against hope until they could pay the brokers no more on that lovely December afternoon.

According to Jhunjhunwala, when commencing to speculate, one should divide one's total affordable loss into ten parts. And risk only one part at a time. Never bank on either a certainty or a hope. Expectation or prediction yes, but no digging in of egos. Anyone could be wrong any time. Even if one had inside information, one could not be certain. Evidently, Nanji Shyamji or their agent in say Hong Kong must have had inside knowledge of the importing department's intention. But they overlooked the border dispute or did not really know about it until it was late. Jhunjhunwala was clear that one might expect the market to go one way, but it could go the other. Say one feels bearish and sells. If prices went up further, tell the broker to cover or cut off the transaction as soon as the one tenth (one of the ten parts one could afford to lose) is lost.

Having been wrong once, wait for another opportunity to take a fresh view and try again but only with one tenth of the money. Even by the rule of statistics one should click right at least one out of the ten possible attempts. When right, keep doubling. If one has bought and the market rises, buy more and more until prices turn downwards. As soon as they do, sell the whole lot and book the profit. In this Marwari approach, either one loses one-tenth of one's fund and starts again. Or when right, one's average cost is lower than the ruling price; one can build up a huge position and expect to make a killing. Jhunjhunwala's contention was that he had studied quite a few failure stories and had found that the speculator had got carried away by pride, over-confidence or obstinacy and had violated the rules of the theory and had doubled and redoubled in loss. A la Nanji Shyamji, as I discovered two years later in 1958.

Had I been able to remain in the jute/gunny trade I might have seen more of the cut and thrust of the bania. Tea had no forward market. The trade was all in ready goods to be paid for within 14 days of sale. The commodity was perishable, its variety was infinite, and speculation was not possible. In the sixties there were few Marwari tea traders. The only Marwaris I could interact with therefore were garden owners. Two men I clearly remember. One was Pawan Kumar Kanoria who headed a department of five or six family owned gardens. He was about my age and yet so much more *au fait* with business. He knew not only about his sphere but also about commerce in general. I felt like a learner in the presence of the experienced. At say 25, he had the maturity to size up situations and exercise choices.

Also, about my age was Bimal Kumar Ganeriwala. He looked after only two family-owned gardens in the Cachar district of Assam. He again was streets ahead of me. Mind you,

I had taken a reasonably early start. I was 20 years and 8 months old when I joined J. Thomas & Co. But in the knowledge of business and finance, he appeared at least ten years ahead. He also had clarity of perception and maturity of judgment which I felt I did not have. He tried to explain the balance sheet to me. I tried hard to understand but kept forgetting what I thought I had understood. And I bet, no one had explained accounting to him. It was all education by instinct superimposed by experience. About this time, I read somewhere that Haridas Mundhra had begun working in his father's business at the age of 8 and by 30 he was acclaimed a genius at acquiring industries and companies. Could it be that an exposure when the brain is at its receptive best makes Marwari boys so much quicker at business understanding? Young girls have the same genes but stay at home and take interest in business, if at all, much later and after marriage. Could it be that they are yet to make an outstanding mark because of the late start?

I just wondered whether those of us non-Marwaris who spent time in schools and colleges were in the same boat as Marwari girls. My colleagues in the tea department did not waste their energy on worrying about such things. The Marwari clients treated them well and in fact deferred to them for representing a British firm. But I was concerned as I was in a comparative hurry to get on, get ahead and also wind up from active business by about the age of 40. Childlike perhaps, but true at the time.

Neither Pawan nor Bimal were by any stretch of imagination stingy. They ran their gardens with a consciousness of cost but were quite liberal in their personal dealings. They were particularly hospitable when I visited their gardens. Without meaning to do so deliberately, I had begun to check on the Marwari reputation, in my mother's family, for miserliness. More so, check on the allegation about their being the Jews of India. While in the gunny department, I had had the opportunity to interact with a number of Jews in the Agarpara Jute Mill owned and managed by BN Elias & Co. In fact, one of the first clients given to me to look after early in 1958 was this Jewish house.

The head of the group was old man Nissim Elias who sat in a medium sized room on an ordinarily decent desk. His daughter, who got married in the course of 1958, sat on a small desk on his right. On the left sat the chief executive of the jute mill as well as the raw jute buyer. Both of them lived in the mill, did their site work early in the morning and then came to the head office in Dalhousie Square (now BBD Bagh) next to the Writers Building. The environment was informal and friendly if not also a little like a marketplace. Although a wealthy man, there was nothing distant or exclusive about Nissim or any of his subordinates. They were all white Jews at BN Elias and had originally come to India from Iraq. Why they were called *white* I never figured out. It was explained to me that it was to distinguish them from the Jews in Maharashtra who were resident in India for many centuries. Why not Iraqi then; why white? Probably to make sure that they were not treated like native Indians by the British in India.

When I began calling on the Agarpara Mill, the gunny sales master and chief executive was one Morris Jonah. Unfortunately, he died within days and was succeeded by David Abraham. A

Philip Raymond succeeded as the jute buyer. They were both friendly, helpful and did not avoid a beginner. Soon I started getting more and more business which gave me an opportunity to interact especially with Abraham. Raymond was a smoker and I used to carry a tin (50) of 555. When he happened to be alone in the room, I offered him a cigarette so that a 15-minute chat became inevitable. Old man Nissim invited me to his daughter's wedding and I presented her with a heavy silver plate out of gratitude for his company giving me a flying start in the gunny trade. In return, Nissim came to my modest wedding party seven years later and gave us a table cigarette box made of silver which we still cherish. My interaction with a few Jews was thus much more than justified by the business.

If they had an obsession, it was their being Jewish. Everything else came later. Money was not such a great priority as would appear from their popular image. During my broker call one afternoon, I overheard Nissim argue a speculative point eloquently with a Marwari trader on the phone. At the end, I bucked up courage enough to pay him a compliment on how very clever he was. How I learnt so much from the conversation. No, my son, no Jew could outdo a typical Marwari at money or speculation, was the old man's answer. He went on to narrate an incident in England. Three Jews bought their three tickets for a train leaving soon. Next in the queue were three Marwaris whom the Jews saw buying only one ticket. When an inspector was seen entering the compartment, all the three Marwaris left their seats and locked themselves in the nearest lavatory. While passing by the inspector knocked at the door. Out came their single ticket from below the door. Happy, the inspector punched and returned it. The envious Jews had caught on with the novel idea. So, on the return journey, the Jews bought only one ticket. The Marwaris purchased none. When the inspector came, the three Jews rushed into the lavatory. A second or two later, the three Marwaris knocked at the door. Out came the single ticket which they took and disappeared into the next lavatory to await the inspector's knock!

Nissim Elias continued now in a more serious vein. We Jews were not allowed to buy land anywhere in Europe. We could not get any form of state employment. So, what were we to do? How were we to survive? Everyone could not be a musician or an artist or a doctor or a lawyer. So, Jews took to trade. And business was limited in those feudal times. Many Jews therefore had to go into money lending, which in turn tended to provoke resentment. Hence the identification of the Jew with money. But the best of our people haven't been businessmen. Albert Einstein and Karl Marx are only two of many examples. If Marx and Leon Trotsky were specimens of a money-minded community, why should they have been anti-bourgeois communists? A number of communists in Russia and elsewhere were incidentally Jewish. In fact, there are few spheres in which Jews have not excelled.

The Marwaris stand out in sharp contrast. They have no supranational loyalty. They are Indians and often staunch ones. While a number of them are patrons of art and music, few of them are well known artists or litterateurs or scientists or politicians. Most of the time, most Marwaris excel in business and show limited interest in other vocations. My father, who worked for Birla Brothers for 37 years, generally appreciated their ethos but occasionally got put off by what he perceived as the Marwari presumption that everyone and everything had a price. Much later in the mid sixties, when I got the opportunity, I posed this proposition to Biswambar Prasad Kedia, the then President of Jayshree Tea & Industries, also a Birla concern. He said that my father had slightly misunderstood the matter.

There was no doubt that the average Marwari loved wealth, Kedia explained. But then, who wasn't attracted by money except a *sadhu* or a *sanyasi?* The difference was that a bania not only loved money but also understood its dynamics instinctively. Moreover, he was dedicated to it. Every man was attracted by a beautiful girl but how many had the dedication to pursue her, persuade her and enjoy her beauty? Not many men, Kedia went on, understood lovemaking. Merely indulging in sex was not lovemaking. That was just getting relief from the sexual urge. Obtaining pleasure from love needed an aptitude for lovemaking. The ancient Hindus were so aware of the difference that they wrote treatises like *Kamasutra* and *Koka Shastra*. They also illustrated the potential for obtaining pleasure by carving on temple walls as in Khajuraho, Konark and Jagannathpuri.

In the good old days, evidently sex was in no way taboo. Women went about freely. They wore saris but there were no blouses, stitched clothes came to India with the Muslims, as did the *purdah*. Much later, with the Europeans, came the Christian preoccupation with the forbidden fruit to India and sex began to go underground until the middle classes began to consider sexual pleasure to be almost a sin. In ancient India, the pursuit of wealth was also considered desirable. The Hindu astrological treatises often used the extent of land, the number of houses, how many bulls and/or cows a person would live to own as the measure of his fortune or otherwise. Apart from the number of sons, the benchmark of a good horoscope was the wealth it indicated. The bania, and the businessman began to be somewhat looked down upon when *trade* began to compete and overtake *land* as a source of wealth.

To go back to the Kedia explanation, the Marwari had the ability to evaluate many things with the common factor of money. Say a holiday whether in Mussoorie or in Switzerland, the pleasure, the cost, the loss of profit in business or profession due to the absence from workplace and the possible loss of future opportunities by being away. The process was intuitive and within minutes it was clear to the man the pros and cons of going to Mussoorie vis-à-vis Switzerland vis-à-vis not going anywhere. This gift made the average Marwari more clear-headed than most people; the corollary was quick decisiveness. As with a holiday, more so with a business proposal, his vision is clear and therefore his mind is quick. Others also study, compare and decide but the process can be slower because it is less intuitive. I have not come across any instance of a Marwari backing out of a commitment because of regret or a change of mind. Backing out due to reasons of opportunity or a change in the market is a different matter.

So much for the average Marwari, there are extraordinary ones also. The best financial mind I had the good fortune to interact with was the late Keshav Prasad Goenka. In my endeavour to understand the basics of finance I had come across a number of accountants. Many could see only the obvious one dimension to a balance sheet. Some specialists could see two dimensions. One or two I had met might have seen say three. KPG could see, as it were, seven. I remember he once asked his experts how much he should pay for the company whose annual accounts he gave them. After a brief study, the expert consensus was, if my memory serves me right, up to Rs 30 lakh. Thereafter, KPG gave his analysis, which as it unfolded, proved quite startling. At the end everyone agreed that the value could go up to Rs130 lakh. I must confess I had silently endorsed the first modest figure. Fortunately, I hadn't had to open my mouth.

KPG was truly exceptional at finance. His empire could have been much greater and could have grown much more. He was, however, a pathological bear and not a bull. He was an implicit pessimist without quite realising it. The other problem was his primary schooling was, as it were, in pre-war speculation rather than post-war industry. And he belonged to a generation which grew up among low taxes. In the Nehruvian era, however, saving tax had become more useful than earning income. To that extent, KPG hadn't adjusted his sights.

All this made KPG careful with money. When he gave an employee a hundred rupees, he could not remember that it cost the company only Rs 40. The balance Rs 60 would be income tax. Yet my nine years with his company were extraordinarily rewarding. Where I had expected a hundred rupees, I was given two hundred. The experience completely contradicted my childhood image of the Marwari as being stingy. True, I had taken much more risk than the normal manager and had been lucky enough to deliver. To that extent, it was an exchange of service for money, of reward for success. But then, take my father's experience and the Birla Ethos.

Paradoxically, why should such an instructively capable and generously charitable community not have a good image?

THE BIRLAS AS EMPLOYERS

MAGANLAL GANDHI told me that joining a Birla group company was like acting in a play or a film. One should do as the director of the drama tells him to. Stand on one's head if one has to. Hypothetically speaking, make love or commit a murder. Play the hero or the villain or the servant or what have you. In effect, do not let one's private preferences or principles impose themselves on one's professional work. Forget oneself and remember only one's role while one is on the stage.

This was in December 1956 and Maganlal was the elder brother of my aunt Vasant's husband. He was then chief executive of Century Mills which the Birlas had acquired a few years earlier. See, I have the glorified title of chief executive officer, he said, but I have no real powers. They have put me here as a sop to the Gujarati sentiment of Mumbai business which had not been happy at the Birlas replacing Sir Chunilal Mehta. I have a not unimpressive career record. A barrister who was the chief justice of Bhavnagar State until it acceded to the Union of India on the morrow of Independence in 1947.

If I had argued about my powers, continued Maganlal, I would not have got the job. How could the Birlas have trusted the restructuring and the running of a textile mill to a retired jurist? Nor could they have made one from their own cadres the CEO of Century at this stage of its takeover history. The cadres then consisted largely of Marwari men of limited formal education although of total commitment to the Birla ethos. I was, therefore, the right man for the right role. But if I had asked for powers, I would have ceased to be the right actor. If Sohrab Modi does not like a role, the story, the play or the film could not be changed. The Director would turn to say, Prithviraj Kapoor, wouldn't he? 'Prafull, you are an ambitious chap and I feel you would be able to subordinate your predilections to your objective and not allow your temper and taste to lead your career as your father has done.'

My father, Dwarkadas, had joined the Birlas in 1944 at the age of 34. He was an economics graduate from the University of Boston and had worked for the princely State of Morvi for eleven years. He had moved from Morvi, situated north of Rajkot in Gujarat, all the way to Calcutta. From the cushy comfort of a princely bureaucracy to the cut and thrust of business management. All because he could not see eye to eye with the merry ways of Yuvaraj (crown prince) Mahendrasinh, although Maharajah Lakhdheersinh was truly a kind and dutiful ruler. Also, with all his interest in public affairs, Dwarkadas could not see princely States lasting indefinitely. If and when the British quit India, the Congress would succeed to power and its policy towards the States was well known.

His changeover from Morvi to Calcutta proved visionary from another angle. 1944 and the following couple of years were the eve of the great Birla thrust for industrial expansion. The rising tide would lift all the Birla boats unimaginably high in a short span of time. All that was needed, according to Maganlal, was for my father to have understood and adjusted to the Birla ethos. We employees should not aspire to reform the ethos but to exploit it to rise as high as possible, get as many rewards as possible and become prosperous. Ours was to do or die, not to question why, Maganlal quoted the old adage. But Dwarkadas was a prisoner of his late father's principles like: nothing should be done because it was expedient unless it was also right. Maganlal went on explaining life and career to me.

I was 19 then and anxious to get off to a start and succeed soon. A few months earlier I had obtained a BA degree from Bombay's Elphinstone College with a low second class in history and political science. As an undergraduate, I had hoped to go to Oxford and simultaneously become a Barrister-at-Law; come back and practice. When going to England did not work out, I felt lost for a few months. Then I decided to seek a business job, which in those days, did not require specific education like in management science. Since my father was with the Birlas, it should have been easier to join them than any other company. Nevertheless, I was keen to check with Maganlal Gandhi for he was an exceptionally clear thinker, a keen theoriser of experience and loved to guide youngsters. Unlike many elders who like to give advice, Maganlal preferred to analyse things for the particular youngster, clarify the pros and cons and then let the chap do as he liked. He was a rare guide and philosopher.

About the only large industrial group where a young man could achieve a meteoric rise was Birla Brothers. In any case, our contacts were few and a virtually automatic entry was possible only here. The House preferred the sons of employees, the background was known, presumably the youngster would be familiar with the ethos and was likely to be more spontaneously loyal than an alien recruit. I should have got a start with Rs 350 per month but it never came about. Either my father was away from Calcutta on duty or his boss GD Thirani was unavailable to interview me as he was traveling. Months went by while I had to kick my heels. By November 1957, I got another appointment which was more attractive. But that was by no means the end of my interest in the Birla ethos and them as employers.

As a matter of interest, I had begun to critically analyse all that I could remember my father had talked about since 1944 in the context of the Birlas. Maganlal Gandhi's simile, about being employed by the Birlas, was like acting in a play, and this was on my mind when I now thought of the subject. After I got employed and began to come in contact with jute mill operators, my interest increased. As a part of my training I was sent to India Jute Mills where I spent three weeks. Through my father's good offices, I got to stay in the Birla Jute Mills for a week. There, the word *padatah* first registered in my mind. But more about this fascinating concept later.

My father Dwarkadas was the first factory manager of Hindustan Motors (HM) at Uttarpara, a suburb of Calcutta. In

1949, I recalled that he, along with his several colleagues, was surrounded and kept confined for an hour or so by a group of the workers. This must be one of the first *gheraos* in the country. The incident had quite an impact on Dwarkadas. Before long, he got himself a licence for a revolver. More importantly, he began to talk about the exploitation of labour. Comparatively, few workers feel unexploited and given the opportunity, few managements desist from exploiting their workers. That was life, but a manager should not be neutral between his management and the trade union. But metaphysical reflections might have driven him to neutrality. That is probably why he was soon enough given another assignment in the same concern.

Having been educated abroad (Boston), Dwarkadas could empathise easily with the representatives of Nuffield Motors, the makers of Morris Oxford cars and the English collaborators of HM, like Mr Jones. Or Mr Jessmore of General Motors (GM) USA; the Bedford truck was a GM product which was also made at Uttarpara. He supported their plea for quality and a thorough inspection before a vehicle was dispatched from the factory. But quality tended to reduce quantity and the padatah or costing was reduced by reduced numbers. The overhead expenses of the company were distributed among the number of vehicles dispatched; the fewer the dispatches, the higher the cost per vehicle.

There was nothing startlingly novel about this. The question was: should a manager fall fully in line with the company owners' preference for padatah and production or should he remain committed to the culture of quality above all? This was perhaps the price that highly-educated men pay. They cannot subsume their personality in the company as an actor does when playing a role in a drama. Dwarkadas could not, whereas many a Marwari manager could as a fish takes to water. It is this ready acceptance or surrender that made another manager rise high in the organisation and not his being a Marwari. The public impression in this regard is unfortunately not correct. Mind you, the source of the impression is probably within the company. For instance, although he did not say it outside, yet Dwarkadas believed that there was a preference for Marwaris in Birla Brothers.

How then was a Mr Chatterjee, a senior colleague of Dwarkadas in his earlier assignment with Orient Paper Mills, also a Birla company? GD Thirani was the Secretary and head of HM for several years. His approach also happened to be educated, analytical and therefore did not always agree with the company's. When his approach clashed with the verdict of the padatah, he was gracefully transferred. Now, he was a Marwari, a traditional loyalist of the Birla family and possibly also a distant relative.

What was true was that most of the young men who joined were either from satellite families or from the Marwari community which in those days did not have a tradition of advanced education. Instinctively, they accepted the Birla ethos and got on with their jobs. Very few of them had either the training or the time to tarry, stand and stare at the ways of the organisation. The non-Marwaris who joined were most often qualified men with some critical faculties. Not that they understood business better than the Babus as the Birla family members were called. Nevertheless, they held their independent views based on their own mindsets.

A few years later I checked out on this issue of quality versus cost or padatah with Maganlal. His opinion was that normally, quality is a supreme factor in a consumer item, be it a motor car or a dhoti. To begin with, at Century Mills he had felt the same way as Dwarkadas. He had felt quite upset at being told by his peers and friends in Mumbai that he (because he was the chief executive) had ruined the exquisite quality of *Paramsukh*, the brand name of the finest dhotis. The power of the padatah was having its say. With a slight drop in quality, the productivity had increased, and the cost of cotton had dropped. Yet the dhotis kept selling as no other mill made even this level of quality. And the profit boomed. Fortunately, Maganlal had not opened his mouth on the subject!

The moral of the story was, continued the wise old CEO, that a shortage enabled everything to sell. On such a sellers' market, the quality need not be perfect. On the other hand, greater production ensured lower costs. After all, the object of business was to make profits, quality was only the means to that end. Quite frankly, at the time, I did not clearly understand the conflicting concepts. They all became clear after I came in contact with Biswambar Prasad Kedia, the President of Jayshree Tea & Industries, also a Birla enterprise.

He was the founder CEO of the company which was started to acquire a small tea estate called Lohagarh in the Terai of the Darjeeling district. Kedia had started life as a junior clerk in Birla Brothers. His education was limited and he spoke only in Hindi and Rajasthani. When he smoked, he used only bidis. A person of simple habits, he was a clear-headed thinker. He knew how to build, run and expand his company, a chief executive superior to most I have ever met. There was rarely a piece of paper on his desk. He appeared always free to see colleagues, visitors. To decide and to be available to direct were his only two functions, he used to stress often. I met him and began to see him weekly as a tea broker. The company I represented in those days, J. Thomas & Co., auctioned most of Jayshree teas.

To call on Kedia was every week an education. I owed a great deal of my understanding of tea to him, and quite a bit of business generally as well. As a taster and broker, I was used to talk about quality. But he soon put the issue into perspective. Consistent profitability was the objective. Depending on the variety (whether high-grown or low) of tea, a balance had to be struck between quality and quantity. Also, if the market is strong, quantity is more important to take full advantage of the boom wherein the price differentials are narrow. When the market is weak and discriminating, make good quality. Remember always that the total production had to keep increasing every year. The idea is to try and ensure that the overhead or fixed cost per kg of tea remains constant in the face of inflation and an inevitable rise in expenses.

But padatah did not stop at dividing the cost of production between overheads and direct costs. It kept fractionalising costs almost infinitely. Each component of material used, its price and how much of it was used and how much wasted. A comparison between the costs incurred by parallel machines or modules revealed such factors. Even the overhead per module was often separated to verify the benefits of productivity. Keeping costs down through increasing production was the central secret of Birla success. During the period the Birlas expanded their industrial empire, this secret proved a visionary magic. Kedia was a devotee of the great Ghanshyam Das Birla. He would seize every leisurely opportunity to talk about the genius of the great man.

A low cost was eternally the best defence of an industrial enterprise. Whereas the importance of quality, Kedia would stress, depended on circumstances at a given time. Only during a slump did quality become all important. Ghanshyam Dasji was able to judge the trend of his time. The economy was expanding, people were acquiring greater buying power and hence the demand for goods would keep rising. What one produced was, as it were, bound to sell whether at a premium or a slight discount. On the other hand, the government policy was to substitute imports rather than launch an export drive which might have needed quality. India was, therefore, a paradise to profit by quantity.

On a Friday afternoon in February 1970, I was calling on Kedia when one of the tea estate managers, Saxena (not his real name) came to pay his respects to the President. I offered to leave but Kedia asked me to keep sitting. The performance had not been satisfactory and Saxena was pulled up. After he left the room, Kedia asked me if I could guess how much this manager cost Jayshrees. I didn't know that. After a little while the President said that Saxena cost rupees eight lakh a year. I nearly fell out of my chair. In those days, one lakh rupees a year was considered well paid. How could it possibly cost so much? was my astonishment. Kedia's explanation was that Saxena's estate should by all accounts earn an annual surplus of rupees 20 lakh. The other estates earned on that scale whereas Saxena produced only rupees twelve lakh. The difference of eight lakh was his cost to the company. The pay and perks were the least important in Jayshrees. What mattered was what a manager helped to earn or not earn!

Inefficient managers were sidetracked or even demoted. A sack was reserved only for the man who put his hand in the till. Dwarkadas never quite absorbed the Birla ethos as we have seen. Yet he was not retired until 1981, when he was 71 years old. All because he had repeatedly proved to be honest, on one occasion, beyond the call of duty. The Birlas were also unusually generous in their rewards. Dwarkadas had retired in 1981 and all his dues had been promptly settled. Several months later, Brij Mohan Birla, GD's younger brother, died. I wrote an obituary in the *Capital* magazine, which we used to publish at the time. About two weeks later, my father was called to his old office and given a cheque for Rs 25,000. Dwarkadas was surprised, albeit pleasantly. But why remained the question. The accountant said Babu (means Ganga Prasad) did not say why, he merely asked me to give the cheque to you. Being an old colleague, however he ventured to guess, probably Babu was pleased with the compliments paid to Brij Mohanji in the *Capital* obituary!

There was another face to the Birlas as employers. During the fifties, when Dwarkadas worked at Uttarpara, the purchase head of HM was one HN Kalani. At some stage soon enough, he was found to be inefficient although not dishonest. Overnight he ceased to be purchase manager and became the storekeeper to work under his own erstwhile young subordinate. Kalani's pay and perks however, remained the same. Years later, when I referred this instance to Kedia, his answer was prompt. Anyone in operational charge has to deliver the goods. Otherwise, he would let the whole company down. He had no right to do that. Security of service and livelihood should not be confused with seniority or security of status. Most companies do that; managers feel very upset if and when superseded. In our setup, Kedia continued, it is responsibility and not seniority. And you cannot deserve responsibility if you are not able to be responsible enough. Most executives find this disconcerting. It seems paradoxical not to reward seniority but reward capability. However, this is where the Corporate world is headed while a 21st century government, which needs capability most, is still anchored to seniority.

BRITISH SUCCESS AT BUSINESS

ON 25 November 1957, it was ten past one when my senior colleague JFC Roger took me down and across the courtyard for lunch. It was a sprawling old building; a marble tablet near the gate called it the former residence of Sir John Clavering, a member of Warren Hastings' council. The lunch table was also old; on it had carved retiring executives their initials. They had evidently used fruit knives, all quite crude and of differing sizes and styles but all historical because the years were also carved below the initials. On the walls were black and white portraits of past *burra sahib*s or chief executives.

Each chair had a typed menu in front of it on the table. The first and main item was a beef dish. The head waiter, a tall impressive chap, soon brought the chunks of beef covered with thick gravy. I quietly took one piece. I had never eaten any kind of meat before. Even an omlette I might have consumed no more than three times in my 20 years. The prospect of the lunch was therefore horrifying; I do not think though that my face reflected the horror noticeably. There were some seven Britons and two other Indians around the rectangular table. By a sheer exercise of will, I cut the chunks of beef and, piece by piece, swallowed a portion of it over the next ten or twelve minutes. I could not chew it, hence I straight gulped the pieces down. The job just meant too much to me and I feared that this company of expatriates would reject me as too native and not confirm my appointment. It was my first day at work. I had hardly met Europeans before. I did not know how they thought and what they would do. All I knew was that I had to hang on to the job dearer than life. Nevertheless, when I left the lunch room to return to my work seat, I felt I had escaped from a torture chamber.

I said the job was to me dearer than life. I had realised what it meant to me because I had lost it once before. I remembered an earlier comment of a friend, fond of literature, that Devdas did not know how much he loved Paromita until he had lost her. J. Thomas & Co. of the then 8, Mission Row, Calcutta had several months earlier held interviews to recruit a youngster to its tea department through which, by far, more tea was auctioned than through any other company in the world. I did not have the kind of contacts necessary to go anywhere near the portals of this essentially British enterprise founded, I think in 1831, and still controlled by a Welsh family called Thomas. But a generous well-wisher, Vinod Parekh, who had happened to have earlier seen me for a few minutes with his nephew Ramesh Parekh, introduced me to the company.

In final round, there were three others. Bheem Varma, a

Doon School boy and at once the nephew of the Maharajahs of Cooch Behar and Tripura, Kamal Bhagat, also an intelligent Doon lad and Akhil Marfatia, a graduate of the London School of Economics and therefore perhaps too educated to be a broker. In business IQ, I imagined I was the best. If anyone happened to beat me, it would Bhagat. But it turned out that he had a brother working for one of the clients called James Warren & Co. He was therefore out – clients' relatives could someday exert extra-constitutional pressures. J. Thomas & Co. therefore, did not employ them.

Since I was introduced by Parekh, the company's number three Director, I got what seemed like a series of fair interviews by several other Directors. The persisting question was which school had I been to. No one enquired which college or university. In my nervousness (my hands used to get colder than ice) and anxiety I did not note the significance of this question. Eventually, I was told that I had been placed second. Varma was selected. Much later I realised that he was the correct choice. The large clients or tea garden-owning companies were headed by expatriates. They felt at ease with and tended to spontaneously trust their own people. The next best was an Indian prince, especially if he had been to a public school whereas it was difficult for an Indian commoner to enjoy a ready entry into the chambers and homes of the British.

Twenty is no age to get consoled with these arguments even if I had known them. For no fault of J. Thomas & Co., I was heartbroken at being rejected. For the four following days I could hardly eat anything, whether at lunch or at dinner. In sympathy, my mother too could not have much food. Several weeks later I was surprised by the arrival of a short letter from Parekh, asking me to phone him. Come and see the company's chairman Guy Routlege. I donned my one and only suit, a fairly heavy woolen outfit, and rushed the same afternoon; I took a taxi to be on time and to enter the office porch respectably. It was 21 November 1957, a Thursday and I was ushered into Routlege's room at 5 pm,

The head of the executive gunny (not tea) department had been hospitalised. The youngest member had earlier resigned and returned to Scotland. And the two remaining men could not cope with the work of four. Routlege asked whether I could join immediately. My reflex reply was: tomorrow morning Sir! That was too early, he replied. What about the 1st of December? But I thought you wanted someone to start immediately, Sir! That was true admitted the big chief and went on to decide on Monday the 25th. Even in an emergency, he was not prepared to appear to flap, it seemed. The 1st of a month was the promptest alternative to the first day of a year. Even 25th was a bit like hustling. Routlege was the son of a distinguished member of the tea fraternity in the City of London. Urbane and aristocratic looking, when in England he played polo with the likes of Prince Philip, the Duke of Edinburgh.

He was slightly apologetic in declaring that, unlike in the tea department, my gunny appointment would carry a 12-month probation because the company did not know how an Indian would fare in the sphere of jute. J. Thomas & Co. had never tried an Indian executive (called a covenanted assistant) before. It was much later that I came to know that the head of the gunny department, covenanted Gay, was dead against trying

Indians as executives. As underbrokers or guarantee banias or clerks and peons they were alright. But the executives had to be Scottish: In its century-long history the jute side of J. Thomas & Co., it had had only one Englishman and one Welshman and that too, a Thomas.

A month with the clerks in the office, a month in the Jute mills and a month going around to the clients' offices with the senior colleagues was adequate education. No matter my emergency appointment, there was no cutting corners on the training. Thereafter, I was given a list of small clients to look after and floated on the market. Came the 1st of April (1958) and my probation ended. I was given a proper three-year contract.

Gay had recovered quickly from his illness and had resumed work much sooner than had been feared. He personally handed over the contract to me. He explained that he had been wrong in objecting to the appointment of Indians. He confessed that he had got prejudiced by the sharp ways of the Marwari jute merchants. Quite uncannily, one of the clients asked Roger the day after I joined work as to why J. Thomas & Co. had employed a Marwari. Perhaps the client was also prejudiced or maybe he was having a crack at Gay's bias. The fortunate outcome was that it dawned on Roger that I could be a vegetarian and promptly told the kitchen that special food should be served to me whenever required.

Yet a more fortunate result was that it evoked a clarification from me that I was not a Marwari; that Garodias were Agarwals from Rajasthan whereas Goradias were from Gujarat. This came as a relief to Gay. He was candid enough to admit that he had opposed my appointment, but he had been overruled by Routlege on the argument that Scottish youngsters were no longer likely to come out to India any way. It was not worth their while and therefore there was no alternative to employing Indians. He was more candid to confess how wrong he was and how well I had done. Hence this early confirmation and contract.

I was delighted, a few days earlier I had completed 21 and was now in my 22nd year. After the flush of joy had subsided, I was struck by a surprise. For all practical purposes, I had no contact with Europeans before joining J. Thomas & Co. I found it difficult to believe that anyone could be so fair and frank. So ready to admit his misjudgment, reverse his views and confide it all to a very young subordinate. Did Gay not have an ego? Or was it that he subordinated his ego to truth and reality?

One evening late in January of 1959, the Directors and the executives of the jute and gunny departments were called down by the burra sahib. Only I was not. Before leaving the room, Roger said that if he was late in returning, I could carry on and go home as usual. Curious as well as slightly cut up at being excluded, I waited until 6.30, hoping to know what the development was. None returned by then and I left for home; not because I was in a hurry but because I did not want to seem a nosy parker. The next morning Roger told me that the meeting did not get over until a little after seven. Since there were no prospects of either the jute or the gunny department doing much better, there was no future. It was therefore decided to close down the two departments, gunny in March 1959 and jute the year after. All the Scotts were to be retired, seven of them in all including four of jute. Strangely, they were surprised if not also shocked at the decision. Yet they were all calm and pleasant as usual the following morning. From the office, they had retired to have a couple of drinks in order to absorb the shock of the decision and to be able to sleep normally that night. And evidently, they had slept well.

There was not the slightest hint of rancour. Mind you, except for two or three of them, they were too old to find good new careers again in the UK. Who would want a jute broker there? Not only no rancour but also no anxiety as to the retirement benefits. The company would surely do them as well as possible. I could not imagine my remaining so calm and sanguine under such circumstances. Because I was told I would be transferred to the tea department, I was able to keep my cool.

There was the other side of this coin of calmness in crisis. The year I joined, the gunny department had grossed an income of Rs 5 lakh. Of this sum, Rs one lac or 20 per cent was as usual paid to the guarantee banias, two Marwari brothers called Almal. While they also helped in looking after clients, the main reason for paying them was for their underwriting any payment or delivery failure by any Indian trader. All British companies that traded with Indians had such guarantee banias, for, the belief was their expatriate executives could not know enough about the creditworthiness of the natives. Any contract that was not direct between the jute mill and the buyer (generally exporter) was called a principal contract. This means that the mill would hold only J. Thomas & Co. responsible. By 1958, the contracts were mostly direct. One of the reasons was the reluctance of the Almal brothers to allow any principal transaction which carried even an iota of risk. What then was the sense in carrying the Almals at a cost of Rs1lakh to a losing department? To which Gay's and Roger's answer was: it would not be fair to discard them after so many decades of association. The implicit message was to try and earn more brokerage if you could. Do not ditch allies and satellites, nor tear up a network. If you were to be unable to cope, accept defeat. Altogether a message surprising to an Indian whose first great instinct is survival, but who, unlike the British, is no pioneer.

The secret of British success at business was rarely genius or competitiveness. It was the pioneering initiative and the loyalty which the British executives gave to their employers. For example, there is no instance of an expatriate hijacking his employer's business. Yes, any number might have put their hand in the till, but none went beyond lining his pocket. On a grander scale, neither Robert Clive nor Warren Hastings ever tried to become the Nawab of Bengal, although they could have.

Paradoxically, character rather than ability was the secret of success.

UNIONIZED STAFF

UNTIL RECENTLY, in Cochin it was difficult to get sufficient work from unionised staff in the office. Our little branch had eleven such staff members. Individually, they were all decent men and when we promoted two of them to junior officers in 1989, their entire attitude changed; and they behaved and worked hard as officers. The other nine continued as before. They would start work exactly at 8 am. At 12.30 pm they would stop work regardless of any urgency and start eating lunch or playing carom. At one o'clock, they would get back to work and at 4.30 they would put their pens down and go home. Even if there was pressure of work on say a tea auction day, they would not lift a finger to help the executives.

Every three years, there would be negotiations with the union and wages would go up sharply. The applicable price index kept ahead of the cost of living and hence usually the wage escalated. Early in 1993, the prices of tea fell and yet the union put up extensive demands. To which our reply was that we could renew the three-year agreement without any change. The union neither withdrew the demand nor pressed for it; the staff behaved as if nothing had happened. Come 1994, the prices improved and the demand was renewed with retrospective effect.

After about three weeks, they began slogan-shouting at the office door before going home. After another three weeks, they put up some buntings and posters so that anybody passing by the office could know that an agitation was going on. The buntings, the flags, the posters and other decorations to attract attention increased progressively. Thereafter, they threatened a one-day strike but did not actually implement it; probably they knew that a strike in a broker's office, unlike an industrial house, was risky for the company. The clients may withdraw their teas and send them to another broker and may not come back.

We realised that if we conceded to an expensive new agreement, the branch might become unviable. Moreover, the wage level would spread to our Coimbatore and Coonoor offices, possibly making our entire south Indian business unviable. Incidentally, the union was averse to conceding any increase in the workload or extending the hours of work. With the staff members' existing work pattern, this was not negotiable.

I, therefore, decided to try a new experiment in industrial relations. We told our Director in-charge of south India to paste a brief notice early in the morning on the following Wednesday to the effect that the office would not open today. The executives stayed away but all the nine unaware staff members came to work as usual. They found the office closed but presumed that the executive with the keys had got delayed on the way. So, they waited while the clock ticked away. As their friends in the neighbourhood asked as to what had happened, by 9.30 am, one or two of the staff members said that in all probability the manager's mother had died and hence the office had not opened. By about 11 o'clock, as we heard later, they got fed up and all nine of them went away.

The next morning different members of the staff, talking to different executives, protested bitterly on their humiliation the previous morning. Some of them even said that the management's action was illegal; to which our answer was that there was no proposal to cut the day's wage. Where was the question of any illegality? Having got the detailed report at Delhi, we followed up by asking the Director to paste a similar notice the following Friday with one change: the office would open at 11.00 am today.

The whole intention was to test the will as well as the patience of the nine yeomen. Humiliation all over again on Friday; they did not know how to answer the neighbours who again enquired as to what had happened. Apparently, a few persons also taunted them as to why they were tolerating such a whimsical management? At 11 am sharp the executives opened the office but when going in they found none of the nine persons. While the executives were settling down at their desks, they heard a few sounds and voices at the rear of the office building. After a few minutes, eight of the nine sheepishly trickled into the office. One of them had gone to the dentist with a bad toothache.

Meanwhile, over this week we had started assuring our

clients that we would sort out the affairs of our unionised staff. They were, therefore, to kindly bear with us for two or three weeks by not sending us any tea to catalogue and auction. When the supply nearly dried up, I proceeded to Kochi without informing anyone except one of our colleagues. Having reached Kochi, I chatted individually with three of our executives to assess the situation. Next morning, I reached the office at 10.30 am. I shook hands with most of the colleagues, executive or otherwise. I asked a few of the nine as to why they were looking downcast. To which one of them replied that there were only two lots of tea, against the normal about hundred, to compile the next catalogue.

At 11.30 am I called a meeting of everyone in the office and addressed them. I said I had come all the way from Delhi merely to persuade our clients to resume sending tea by assuring them that our staff agitation would be over soon: in any case our staff members were so responsible that their action would pose no danger to the safe sale of teas. So, they were to try not to worry.

However, we had made one blunder and that was to display our wage dispute for the whole world to see. We need not have put up all the buntings, flags, posters and other colourful decorations. Nor should they have shouted slogans outside the office premises. Instead of trying to embarrass the management by going public, they had frightened the clients. I asked Vincent, the stenographer, as to whether he had ever had a fight with his wife. He said a few times. Then, after fighting, did he run outside to tell all his neighbours that he had quarreled with his wife? To which Vincent answered, no Sir, how could I do that? That would damage the family reputation. Then I asked Nair, the cashier, whether he had ever had a dispute with his father. His reply was, once or twice. After the argument with his father, did he inform his friends and neighbours about his differences with his father? He said, of course not.

Then my question to everyone was why on earth had they advertised so loudly the dispute over wages between the union and the management? For all the differences are confined only to two parties, the management and the union. Most of the staff members felt embarrassed at my question but said nothing. I then said, anyway what has happened is done, now let us try our best to recover. Do you agree? And everyone said, yes. I am personally hopeful, I declared. At the same time, let us take a precaution. Everyone here should this evening or tomorrow morning inform his family about this development. Tell them that if Goradia succeeds in reviving the business, well and good. But fails and the branch closes down, all of us will be offered a transfer to different places where the Company has business. One or two may go to Kolkata. Someone may have to go to Guwahati, someone else to Coonoor and so on. There is no threat to your job. If anybody happens to have a special problem due to children or due to parents or any other reason, he may request the Company for a decent hand-shake so that he can stay back with his family in Cochin. Then wishing everyone good luck, the Director and I proceeded to the nearby Taj hotel for lunch. I said to our Malayalee colleagues to join us after having heard the staff's reaction, if any.

Before one o'clock, the senior-most colleague turned up at the Taj and told us that all the nine had come to him and asked the management to name one uniform figure of compensation to all the nine. If the offer was satisfactory, they would consider leaving rather than working for an uncertain future. I sent the colleague back with an all in one figure of Rs 177,777 to each of the nine, plus provident fund. In my opinion, I said, this figure would be lucky for the management as well as the staff. I was not prepared to bargain as I was a believer in the science of numbers. Take it or leave it and carry on working. Within the next nine days, all the nine yeomen had taken the figure offered, said goodbye and left.

It was a psychological googly that dismissed nine batsmen rather than either law or muscle. The paradox is, in unviable situations, psychological operations work better but few industrialists in India think it out, the usual practice is crude – protests, lockouts, shutdowns, losses, police muscle and everything else that will make for economic disaster rather than solutions.

POLITICAL PREJUDICES

URDU

A LOT of pessimism has been expressed about the future of the Urdu language. While I may not share this pessimism, I do realise that it is not going to be hunky dory for it. I recognise the hurdles that lie in its path of survival. At the same time, one should appreciate the inherent qualities of Urdu.

Agreed, the language is probably unique in not having a territorial root. Qaid-e-Azam Jinnah chose it as the language of Pakistan in 1947 not because it was the tongue of any of the provinces that formed the new country. Even in the Punjab, Urdu was the medium of education which in turn was largely confined to the intelligentsia. The common man spoke only Punjabi which incidentally did not have a script. The Gurmukhi alphabet became current in the Punjab after Partition.

With the rise of Punjabi chauvinism and of the discrimination against the *mohajir*s, it is difficult to predict the popularity of Urdu in Pakistan. Nevertheless, it is most sophisticated of the tongues in the country. And there is not much literature in Punjabi. At the same time, Urdu has over the last 50 years become widely understood in India but today there exists some political prejudice. With the spread of education in Hindi, even in Uttar Pradesh, Urdu has been driven to a rear seat.

Even in the heydays of the Muslim League in Uttar Pradesh, the common folk spoke the local lingo whether Bhojpuri, Poorvi, Awadhi or Brajbhasha. In the context, Urdu was at the best of times, the language of the classes and more so of the Muslim classes.

It must, however, be admitted that whenever a Muslim hears Urdu spoken by a non-Muslim, his eyes sparkle. I have experienced this with Muslims from Maharashtra, Gujarat as well as Malabar in Kerala. None of these people I spoke to knew the language, but they were delighted to hear me speak. Some of them, I suspected, felt as if I identified with them.

In my observation over the decades, there are three peoples who are particularly sentimental about their tongues: the Bengalis, the Tamils and the Muslims in India. There are still some old Hindus in the Punjab and Uttar Pradesh whose first language is Urdu. But they do not carry their love for it, as it were, on their sleeves. The Muslims do; to that extent Urdu is a Muslim language and a vehicle of their identity.

There are exceptions, of course. The Bengali Muslims, as a sweeping generalisation, do not like Urdu. They resent it as a rival to their own beloved Bangla. Admittedly, the Bengali Muslim is somewhat of a schizoid. I do not mean to be derogatory but merely to stress that he has a tendency to swing like a pendulum between Islam and Bengaliness.

Within months of Independence, East Bengal reacted to Qaid-e-Azam Jinnah's choice of Urdu as the Pak national language. There was widespread agitation in Dhaka (then Dacca). The objection gathered strength with the passage of years. There also gathered many other grievances against the western wing. And eventually the country broke up when Bangladesh became independent in 1972.

Uncannily, its army of liberation was called *MuktiBahini*, so very Sanskrit in origin. No thought was given to naming it after jihad (*Mujahideen-e-Bangla* or some such expression) as is the Islamic proclivity elsewhere. Urdu was distanced, if not totally abolished. It was an alien tongue of tyrants from the western wing. And soon, the radio and the TV said *aakaashpaataal*.

After Sheikh Mujibur Rahman was assassinated and succeeded by Zia-ul-Rahman, Bangladesh was declared an Islamic Republic. Among the many perceptible changes was the switch by the radio and the TV to *aasmaanzameen*. Bangladesh swung a full 180 degrees to the Islamic end. Not for the first time though. We should not forget that the Muslim League, the champion of the partition, was founded in Dhaka in 1906.

In 1947, Fazlul Haque had suggested to Sarat Bose (Netaji's brother) the idea of a united Bengal separate from India or Pakistan. Yet the year (the 1946 election) before, most Muslims of Bengal had voted for the League and its demand for Pakistan. The League's Direct Action to secure Pakistan was launched in Calcutta on 16 August 1946. This was the biggest single Hindu-Muslim riot until then! What a paradox, voting for Pakistan and wanting a united and independent Bengal!

Enough of the deficiencies of Urdu for the time being. Let us look at its strengths. I am no linguist. Nevertheless, I find it difficult to believe that any other tongue has a wider range of sounds. In the context, the language is indeed a grand piano. Its alphabet represents every sound in Arabic, Persian and Hindi.

The only letters that I can think of as missing are the second 'L' of Gujarati and Marathi and the special 'Rh' of Tamil usually spelt as 'I ZH' as in Kozhikode, the indigenous version of the anglicised Calicut. There must be a few other missing sounds which I do not know about.

The nouns and the adjectives are Arabic, Persian or Hindi but the verbs are all Hindi. The grammatical base built on Hindi or *khadi boli,* as it was known when Urdu was evolving. Incidentally, the tongue also has some Turkish words such as Urdu itself, which is Turkish for army, troops, or *lashkar*. This might probably be because it began as a bridge of communication between the foreign soldiers and the local populace.

Urdu has the force of Arabic, the symphony of Persian and both mellowed by the sweetness of Hindi. I can lay no claim to scholarship in this or any other language. But I have spent several hundred hours and many thousand rupees trying to learn spoken Urdu. My object was to be able to pronounce and speak Hindustani correctly; not to learn Urdu per se, nor to appreciate *shaairi* (poetry).

My teacher or *ustaad* for most of the years between 1977 and 1986 was Agha Iqbal Mirza, a graduate in English from the then Delhi College. His grandfather had been the *kotwal* of Delhi, probably a legacy from the Mughal era which happened to be deferred to by the British government. The point I am making is that Mirza had at once old pedigree and modern education to help me.

My own aptitude for languages is limited. Most of my eight-year formal education was confined to English. Yet my pronunciations in Bengali, Gujarati, Hindi and Urdu, my listeners have told me, are reasonably authentic. Which means I might have a sense of sound; quite paradoxically I happen to be almost deaf when it comes to appreciating music. My views are based on these traits and not on any depth of knowledge.

One thing is certain. The Hindi or the Bollywood film will lose its élan if Urdu were not to play its active role. True, mythological movies have flourished on pure Hindi. The credit there should go to the power of the themes and the readiness of the Hindu masses to relate to them. But what of the social and other films? How would their dialogues tick without at least some Urdu words? If an early example is *Mughal-e-Azam*, a recent example is *Raazi.*

Then what about the music? The *ghazal* is the very cornerstone of the Hindi film song. The *geet* alone cannot carry it. Nor can every movie sell without songs. From Hollywood, a musical was a specialty, whereas from Bollywood, a non-musical is an exception. And there is a magic to a movie from Mumbai or else it cannot be such a successful industry.

Contrast its success with the performance of Tollywood or the Bengali film made in Tollygunge studios. Calcutta has given Bollywood more artistes than Mumbai. Yet the same Bengali artistes could not fire the Indian imagination from Tollygunge as they could from say, Chembur (Mumbai). After all, Bengalis also see Hindi films. And Bengali movies could have been either dubbed in Hindi or re-filmed on a grander scale.

But no such luck. Not even for the matinee record makers like *Chandidas* of the good old days, *Saat Paake Bandha* or *Pather Panchali* of yesteryears or *Gupi Gayen Bagha Bayen* and *Unisey April* of recent vintage. This is all merely to stress the influence of Urdu over films in India and therefore its strength.

The script is Urdu's greatest handicap. It is an opaque curtain that keeps out most Indians from learning the charismatic tongue. And charismatic it indeed is. Even those who do not understand it at all, like to hear its sound. If Urdu could be read in say the Roman script, it would spread like wildfire and delight people as if they were warm in a snow bound region. But then, many a maulvi would say, Urdu would lose its *rooh* or soul! Paradoxical indeed!

AHMED ALI JINNAH

OVER THE years, some among my acquaintances possibly might have reason to harbour reservations regarding my attitude towards Muslims. It is best I write to explain not only my viewpoint but also my experience to back it up. Perhaps I might succeed in putting across to the reader a thing or two about the Muslim community in India.

First of all, I wish to declare that I am not against the Muslims. Years ago, one Vakeel Khan came to us and stayed with us. All of us became very fond of him, and he did us proud indeed. He died while my mother and I were taking him to Moolchand Hospital in Delhi. And what a send-off to Ghazipur we gave his body. I have not yet wept at any death except Vakeel's. The memories he has left behind still haunt me and how I wish more people could be as wonderful as him.

For a long-retired butler of the Bengal Club, it could not have been easy for him to fit into our household. He did, because he was keen to be in Delhi. But he could also because we made him so welcome and wanted. He adored the British and often got nostalgic about some of the expatriate sahibs who stayed at the Bengal Club. About the only Indian he could condescend to look up to was Jawaharlal Nehru, who he said was a *raees* and not entirely different from a *sahib*.

You may appreciate how resplendent he often used to look. His Afghan posture, his blue eyes, his well-trimmed beard all stood out when he wore my maternal grandfather's old dinner jacket converted into his bund gala suit topped with his black Banarsi cap. It was as though an etching on silver had been framed in black to highlight its splendour. Once Partha and Kalyani Gupta, both offspring of ICS officers, mistook him at our dinner for the chief guest! Although Vakeel Khan kept a beard, he shaved his upper lip. This showed his commitment to the Islamic tradition.

Vakeel and I had many a longish conversation on a number of subjects including the need for Hindu-Muslim unity. He was very reasonable on most issues. On two points, however, he was stubborn. He never agreed with me that the Partition was a mistake or a setback at least for the Muslims who remained in India. Even to a suggestion in the newspapers that the Babri edifice could be converted into a museum as a compromise, his reaction was negative. Yet he looked upon me not only as an employer but also a friend.

My first contact with a Muslim, though, was when I was nine. The gentleman was Ahmed Ali Jinnah, younger brother of the Qaid-e-Azam. The months were June, July and September of 1946. August was largely missed because of the Great

Calcutta Killing and its repercussions in Bombay. Ahmed was a friend of my maternal grandfather, Dharamdas Vora who lived at 401 Girgaum Road, incidentally a Hindu locality in the heart of south Bombay. Ahmed Ali was so fond of Dharamdas' company that he would arrive there in the afternoon and stay up to six. I was impressed by his dress, usually grey trousers and a matching sports jacket, necktie and all. I still remember his gold-rimmed expensive glasses. He often brought with him tit-bits like *kachoris* and *ganthia*. Dharamdas provided the tea and the two of them chatted in engrossment. If I happened to wander into the large third floor *divankhana*, my presence was casually ignored, and I listened into all that Ahmed Ali said.

Except for the hot riot days of August, Ahmed Ali came during most of the weeks when my father Dwarkadas, mother Manjula and I happened to be visiting our grandfather. On one September day, a passenger in the tramcar asked him whether he was not Mr Jinnah. The atmosphere was still charged, and Ahmed Ali was nervous. Fortunately, the passenger decided that it could not be him; how could such a big leader be traveling in a tramcar? Yes, Bombay of those days still had tramcars. The brothers had a striking resemblance of appearance. Ahmed Ali took the risk perhaps also because he was lonely. His Swiss wife and their daughter had left him a few years earlier. And he lived a life of leisure on the six hundred rupees (quite a handsome sum in those days) his brother gave him every month.

Possibly, half seriously and half in jest, Ahmed said several things about his distinguished brother Mohammed Ali. I still recollect some of what I had overheard. Much else I happened to listen into when my grandfather repeated what Ahmed had said during the afternoon to the rest of the family at dinner. According to him, Mohammed Ali was no real *hamdard* (sympathiser) of the Musalmans. If he was, why did he marry a Parsi girl? Why did he not know how to do *namaz*? Why did he drink? And so on.

All he really cared for, according to his brother, was becoming a *badshah* or king. (I don't mind being the Prince of Pakistan was Ahmed's plea for himself!) And many of his minion supporters and some of his Khoja friends, all businessmen, flattered the leader's ego and swore by Pakistan. The name Habib kept coming up quite frequently. They were unhappy at having to compete with the Banias and the Parsis in Bombay. If there was to be partition, they would enjoy virtual monopoly in Karachi, without any Hindu competition. There would be only Punjabi and Sindhi farmers to vie with in business. Incidentally, 16 out of the much-talked-about 22 big business families of Field Marshal Ayub Khan's Pakistan were Gujarati-speaking, namely either Memon, Khoja or Bohra.

Late in September 1946, we returned to Calcutta as usual by train. Because the situation was tense and riot-prone, Dwarkadas' friend Dhirajlal Doshi received us at Howrah station. He had brought with him his friend Kakubhai Thakkar because the latter had a car, a 10 horsepower Ford Anglia. As we came out of the platform area, on the cobbled street we saw several tanks rumbling past. That made the atmosphere more fearsome than it might have been. The bloodiest Hindu Muslim riot that had ever taken place was in Calcutta on 16, 17 and 18 August.

The reports I heard or overheard about the murder and

arson were bloodcurdling. One kept hearing about the riot, which was still continuing in several sectors of Calcutta, as being the Direct Action of the Muslim League. Many years later it was explained to me that the 'Action' was Jinnah's way of declaring to the British as well as the Congress that the two separate nations – that were the Muslims and the rest of Indians – could not coexist; that there was no alternative to the partition of India.

On 15 August 1947, Partition became a reality. Yet there were flags and buntings all over Lake Terrace, the lanes in south Calcutta. Almost every flat had a large national flag in its balcony. Our place did not have a balcony, yet we had unfurled a silk tricolour which my father had bought the previous day for I think Rs 15, equivalent probably to today's Rs 1,000 or more. The people who passed Lake Terrace that day all seemed delighted. Most children had tiny paper flags pinned on their chests. As they walked about or played, they looked to check whether their tiny flags were securely in place. Such was the gaiety I witnessed from the window sil on which I sat with a sleeveless pullover on.

I had been running slow fever for several months. I did not go out all day as was usual for me through those months. But in the evening, my father and mother insisted that we all go out to see the illuminations. My father's colleague in Birla Brothers, Mr Gaur brought the company jeep, a US army veteran of the Burma front in World War II. For the evening, Mr Gaur had taken the hood off so that from the open jeep we could watch Calcutta celebrating what turned out to be its brightest night ever. Before that, the city was a property of the British rulers and soon after that it turned into a receptacle for the hapless refugees who began to stream in from East Pakistan.

As we passed through Rash Behari Avenue, Lansdowne Road, Hazra Road, the air was full of the cries of Jai Hind, the favourite slogan of Netaji Subhas. When we proceeded to Park Circus, Entally and Dharamtollah, we saw Urdu-speaking Muslims sprinkling water that mostly had the fragrance of roses. Azadi Zindabad, Hindustan Zindabad were two of the slogans we heard. Strangely, the third was Qaid-e-Azam Zindabad. We in the jeep imagined that probably the same men wielded knives instead of the sprinklers on 16 August a year ago. Maybe we were quite wrong, but the riots had given us a mindset. The Bengali-speaking Muslims were rarely mentioned in an adverse light.

At the age of ten, I might not have been quite so aware of Partition and its tragedy, but for my father, who worked for the Birla Brothers, it was a time of disquiet. It was widely feared that when the (Radcliffe) Commission had drawn the dividing line, between what was to remain of India and what was to turn into Pakistan, Calcutta was likely to be lost. Correspondingly, Lahore was expected to be in India. It could be more expedient therefore to set up Hindustan Motors somewhere in Gujarat rather than in Uttarpara near Calcutta. My father was deputed to explore a suitable spot or two near say, Baroda. That was how we were in Bombay during 1946 and happened to see Ahmed Ali Jinnah.

Little wonder that my father would often discuss the many implications of Partition and, I used to listen in, a little precociously. Anyway, on 15 August I was depressed, quite likely because of the fever which was not leaving me for several months. And there appeared no distinct hope of its leaving. No doctor was able to diagnose the cause. In the process, I must confess I thought of the tragedy of the country being divided and little about a people being released from slavery. The blame was squarely laid at the door of the Muslim, if not also all Muslims.

In May 1956, I went on a month's tour organised by the Youth Hostels' Association of India. I had taken my final BA examination of the University of Bombay and was all set to relax as well as to enjoy myself. The focus of the tour was Kashmir, although we did stop in Delhi and Amritsar. We were 75 of us in all traveling by a class III railway coach. Five were teachers, two young doctors, about 25 girls and the rest boys. Among the many friends I made, two happened to be Muslims. Sher Ali Dhala was one of the two young doctors while the other was a BSc student of St Xavier's. His name possibly was Basheer something. Both were Khojas from East Africa, both very urbane and well-bred.

It so happened that during the spare hours, the three of us were often together, shopping, riding ponies or walking about in Srinagar, Pahalgam and Gulmarg. There was nothing distinctly Muslim about my two companions or their appearance. Yet the locals of the Valley could make them out. Their lack of Urdu also made no difference. In the bargain, the shopkeepers, the waiters, the drivers, the pony syces spoke to them frankly, giving them their candid feedback. I was overlooked or mistaken for a Muslim; effectively, my presence did not distort the candour of the feedback.

To most of the Valley men, we were from India and they were

Kashmiris. We were welcome as customers and tourists but not as fellow countrymen. Basheer tended to sympathise with this separatist attitude, but Sher Ali was one with India, although I think he held a Tanganyikan or a British subject passport. He would argue as to why did then Kashmiris welcome India's help against the Pakistani invaders in 1947? They should have surrendered and merged with Pakistan. Sheikh Abdullah was, in fact, one with Maharajah Hari Singh in seeking New Delhi's military intervention.

Some of the shopkeepers were clever and charming conversationalists. One of them, I still recollect, replied by asking whether it was right to kidnap a damsel because she had sought your help in distress? To which Sher Ali's retort was but there is surely a difference between *nikah* (marriage) and kidnapping. The Kashmir Maharajah had signed the Instrument of Accession with Sheikh Abdullah approving of the action.

The debates were often interesting, but the fact was that across most of the places we visited, the opinion was for a separate Kashmir, not a merger with Pakistan which was bitterly resented for the loot, rape and arson perpetrated by the invaders. The pony syces at Pahalgam were the exceptions; they seemed to be for India. Maybe their leader was linked with Bakshi Ghulam Mohammed who was then the chief minister.

On return to Calcutta in June 1956, I joined the Hindu Mahasabha. Whether I had reacted to the Kashmir story or had made a positive choice is difficult to tell. All I can say is that through life subsequently, I have seldom taken a decision on the rebound as it were. At the end of 1957, I got employed and there was little leisure thereafter to work for the Mahasabha, which incidentally was becoming inactive. Years went by without much contact with Muslims, except for a chance meeting with Maqsood Ahmed, the grandson of the famous Sir Syed Ahmed Khan, the founder of Aligarh Muslim University.

I was sailing back from Europe (Genoa) on a Lloyd Triestino boat named *M.N. Victoria* during June 1961. On board happened to take place a ping-pong tourney where I had Maqsood Ahmed to play with. He thrashed me, if I remember right, 21:6, 21:8 and as a gracious winner he offered me a cold drink over which we chatted. He was, as I said, grandson of Sir Syed Ahmed Khan.

He told me he had been for many years in Calcutta where I was based. I asked him why he had left such a hospitable city for Karachi. Essentially for one reason, he replied. In the Imperial Tobacco Co (as ITC was then called), he was number 21. On crossing over to the newly formed Pakistan Tobacco Co., he rose to become number 4. He was all smiles and went on to say that soon after *M.N. Victoria* docked at Karachi, he would be taking over as the chief executive officer, a crown he might never have worn had he stayed back in India.

Maqsood Ahmed gave a number of other examples of ICS and other bureaucrats as well as of military officers who got the benefit of meteoric promotions. Those who had witnessed riots or experienced the fear of them would have migrated in any case. The politicised members of the Muslim elite probably considered it their Islamic obligation to migrate. For the rest it was a journey to a land of opportunity. That was the message I received from this grandson of the first known leader who exhorted his Muslim brethren to take to Western education.

Maqsood was as modern and urbane as any aristocratic Indian. He was most probably an Oxonian; if not, a Cantabian. His wife was from an equally cultured background. They made an exceptionally handsome Westernised couple. He could narrate jokes and stories in Hindustani as fluently as in English into the early hours of the morning. Incidentally, she wore only saris on all the days we were on the ship and no *salwar kameez*. Traveling on the ship with us were Smita Divan's* friend, Tritty (then Buhariwala) and the Adarkars. BN later rose to be Governor of the Reserve Bank of India. In fact, we were along with the Maqsoods, as it were, in the same group and socialised on most evenings.

On another evening over whisky, we again got talking about Partition, the Indo-Pak tensions and of the future of the subcontinent. As he saw it from Karachi, the fault was largely Indian. If Pakistan did anything silly, it was out of fear. He swore that every conscious Pakistani was mortally afraid of the giant neighbour. In his view, India practiced double standards and hence even greater fear. Mind you, Maqsood's expressions were impeccably civil and polite.

India took the so-called 'action' in Hyderabad and dethroned that princely State's Nizam because the majority of the people were Hindu. Then, what was wrong in Pakistan sending *mujahideen* into Kashmir in order to take over the State and remove the Maharajah? Hyderabad was not the

---

* Smita Divan was President of the Maharashtra State Women's Council and wife of Constitutional expert Anil Divan.

only instance; there was Junagadh as well. The people from the neighbourhoood rushed into the Nawab's territory and made him flee in an airplane because he had joined Pakistan, Maqsood argued. Most of his compatriots believed, he said, that for Delhi it was a case of heads I win, tails you lose.

Being only 24 and addressing a senior person of 45 or more, I made sure I was particularly courteous. India, I said, does not look at the issue as Hindu and Muslim. It looks at it as (Muslim) Leaguers versus the rest. If, therefore, Delhi considers amalgamating Hyderabad and Junagadh as its right, so does it think Kashmir too is its rightful part? The proof of this contention is the fact that comparatively few Muslims have emigrated out of India, I pointed out. Whereas most Hindus were chased out of Pakistan, especially its western wing.

Maqsood's answer to this was: none really chased anyone out. There were riots and threats in Pakistan as well as in India. It was just that the Muslims stood up to the pressures and fewer of them left their homes. Whereas the Hindus were soft, abandoned their homes and left for India. They could not or did not choose to stand up to the hostile atmosphere until the hostility died down. He did not believe that any systematic effort was undertaken in Pakistan to throw out the Hindus. No more than in isolated pockets of India. True, Punjab had burned for a while. But then East Punjab had hardly any Muslims left by 1948, he pointed out.

I submitted that Nehru's Congress was secular whereas Jinnah's League was exclusively Muslim. The whole ethos in India was based on the equality of all religions before the state; if anything, concessions were made to the non-Hindus.

Pakistan, on the other hand, was essentially a Muslim state. Maqsood could not see the point. Secularism was to him baloney (he did not use this word then but in another context and I suspect, he meant it). If I remember right, he once called Nehru's secularism the Abul Kalam Azad strategy. My next serious encounter with a Muslim was sixteen years later.

Paradoxically, Ahmed Ali Jinnah never went to Pakistan and died in Bombay within two months of his friend Dharamdas' death on the first Independence Day.

A MUSALMAN THINKS

MY LESSON in conversational Urdu would finish for the evening by about 7.30. It was cool, being early December (most probably 1977) and I offered, for the first time, my teacher Ahmed Khan a whisky soda. He was a normally modern person who wore trousers and bushshirts; an undergraduate who spoke English fluently. In the course of the chat over the drink, he happened to call Sheikh Abdullah an opportunist for having made up with New Delhi and become the Chief Minister again. I did not agree with Khan and went on to say that perhaps Sheikh Sahib had realised that Islam could not be the basis of a modern state; Pakistan had not held together and had broken up in 1971. Moreover, the Sheikh might have also reconciled himself to Kashmir being too small to be an independent republic; hence perhaps his release from prison and return to power.

Ahmed felt that the breakup of Pakistan had been engineered

by New Delhi and had, therefore, no lesson to teach on Islam as a basis of a state. Fair enough, that was his view. Our debate was calm and easy through the second *chhota* peg. Thereafter, Ahmed seemed to get animated to tell me that Islam was 'no joke'. It was the most comprehensive code for human life. Sooner or later, it would spread to every nook and corner of the world. It was the most modern prescription. It gave property and inheritance rights to women 1,400 years ago. I listened with interest because he was talking with conviction. Although, I did enquire as to why there was a widespread impression that in orthodox Muslim families, women were not taught much beyond reading the Holy Quran and saying their prayers.

Ahmed got provoked to become more forceful. He asserted that the great faith had an extraordinarily integrated strategy. The cornerstone was fellow feeling, brotherhood and unity. The purpose was to carry Allah's message to all mankind. And it is the simple folk who were likely, in large numbers, to welcome the message. Education was, therefore, not of overriding importance. In fact, too much of it was likely to induce debate, dispute and dissidence.This was what happened to Christianity. A simple dedicated mother is likely to ensure simple faithful children and rear more children cheerfully than an educated woman.

Numbers were a key to making the acceptance of the message universal. Hence family planning was not permitted. Polygamy could only help numbers, Ahmed went on. Often it made the need felt for aphrodisiacs of which the Unani school of medicine had the best variety. Whether this was true or not, I am still not sure, but my animated teacher certainly aroused my interest in the Muslim frame of reference.

Until that fascinating evening, my interest in learning how to speak simple Urdu was merely to be able to pronounce Hindustani words better. For my school final or matriculation in 1952, I had elementary Hindi as an additional subject. But that had not enabled me to speak the language either correctly or fluently. I had heard that the gateway to a good beginning was through Urdu. So, when my intention to eventually shift from Calcutta to Delhi began to crystalise, I began to look for a teacher probably about the middle of 1977. I had no contacts suitable for finding a modern educated Muslim who knew and also could teach me how to speak Urdu correctly. A *maulvi* would be traditional and unfamiliar with the kind of subjects I could chat about. Moreover, he might not have the English to translate for me.

One afternoon, the publisher of an Urdu journal in Patna, a Mr Zaman, dropped into my office. His object was to get to know me and then seek advertisements. I happened to remember and requested him to recommend a suitable Urdu teacher. The result was a call from Ahmed Khan a few days later. He claimed he was of Afghan origin although he was of a slight build and no more than 5 feet 3 inches tall. He had pleasant manners, was a quick wit and an interesting conversationalist. He had a wife, two daughters and a son and, therefore, needed to do business. He hoped to get a contact or two through me more than the salary I proposed to pay him.

Soon began my education in conversational Urdu. Ahmed would come to the house at my convenience and spend an hour or two just chitchatting. I spoke most of the time and he corrected my mistakes; also helped with new words and expressions. If I remember right, some time the following year he began talking of his uncle (*mamu*) who was a senior doctor in a public hospital in Karachi. How much better off people were in Pakistan. That he was in acute need he had told me frequently. We used to help, including with old clothes and things for his children but charity could not take anyone far. One evening Ahmed looked delighted as he declared that he had obtained the visas and the family was migrating to Karachi for good. Before eventually leaving, he was gracious enough to introduce to me an acquaintance of his. Agha Iqbal Mirza would now take Ahmed's place as my Urdu *ustaad* (teacher).

Mirza made it clear soon enough that unlike Ahmed Khan, he was a Moghul; his ancestors came to India not from Afghanistan but from Uzbekistan. Babur had set off from Samarkand in the same region. He was a BA from Delhi College later known as the Maulana Azad College. His grandfather had been, in his day, the *kotwal* (police chief) of Delhi, presumably of only the Shahjahanabad area. He had begun life as an agent of a private airline of which there were many in the 1940s of Calcutta and eastern India. Mirza had not done well in business. Nevertheless, he was upright, honest and quite proud. He preferred to dress in a lounge suit with a bow tie. In Calcutta, he lived with his two brothers and a sister; all the four siblings had never married! In the intellectual sphere, Agha Iqbal had translated a bunch of Urdu short stories into English. The work was published by the Writers Workshop of Professor P Lal, a well-known Calcutta personality.

I could go on talking to Mirza for hours and we tried to meet at least twice a week when I was not travelling out of Calcutta. He corrected my mistakes and tried to explain the origin of words. The verbs were all from *khadi boli* or Hindi as used in the western districts of UP like Agra. The grammar was Hindi except for the plural which often depended upon whether the noun was of Arabic or Persian origin. More than one *sanam* (beloved) was *asnaam*, plural of *khabar* (news) *akhbaar*. That was Arabic. Nouns of Persian ancestry like *khayaal* (thought) became *khayaalaat*. Urdu was indeed a grand piano with a wider range of sounds than any other language. It had two Ks (or a K and a Q), two Khs, two Gs, two Hs, two Js and four varieties of Zs. Mirza was able to make me realise all this and more without my learning a single letter of the alphabet to read or write. He often gave glimpses of esoteric expressions. For instance, *intezaar* was a common word; *muntezir* or the person waiting was less common; but *munltezar* or the awaited person was very rarely used and most people were perhaps unaware of its existence.

Although Mirza did not drink, he had quite a modern, unorthodox outlook. He did feel though that all Muslims should fast during the Ramzan month. But he himself did not, as he had crossed the age of 60. He had no regrets about not having been to Pakistan. He said he had heard that in that country, dogs were fed well but were not allowed to bark. In India, it was the opposite. One could say or speak what one liked, but conditions were poorer. This probably reflected his preoccupation with his own debt and penury. One of the few traits he shared with Ahmed Khan was an implicit presumption that the society owed him a living. As if the world was bound to keep him comfortable. If he was not well off, the fault lay less with him and more with the people around him. I somewhat resented both my teachers for this attitude. When I thought I had hit upon the possible explanation for this presumptuousness many years later, my pique subsided.

The curiosity aroused then led to a continual search for the answer. Only recently did it occur to me that the Judaic ethos tends to assume that God made people equal. It is the imperfect environment on earth which makes them unequal. Society lacks equity. The leaders or the better off, richer people, therefore, often bear an uneasy conscience about the poor and the miserable. Little wonder that European and American visitors to India are shocked by the misery of the poorest Indians. They find it difficult to reconcile themselves to the sharp contrast between the rich and the poor. By the same token probably, the lesser to do among Christians or Muslims consider it their right to be helped by the society which makes them unfortunately unequal.

Khan and Mirza expected the world to help them on this implicit feeling. Maybe so, but I did not get an opportunity to get the point clarified. What emerged from these thoughts was that liberty and equality stand at opposite ends. The slogan of the French Revolution, liberty equality fraternity, has perhaps helped to conceal the contradiction. Or at least delay a debate. Liberty means freedom, for example, to earn, save and bequeath as much as one can. Equality, on the other hand, requires that the earnings are distributed either voluntarily or through social or state intervention. Like progressive income tax whereby the more one earns, the higher the rate of the levy.

Christianity spontaneously tried to narrow the differences between the rich and the poor with the help of social services like free or near-free education and medical care. The schools, colleges and hospitals run by the missionaries like the Society of Jesus come to mind. Islam has its system of *zakaat* whereby every Muslim is required to donate annually two and a half per cent of his wealth. The money raised is to be redistributed to the Muslim poor.

The Hindu ethos is based on *karma* and *Bhagya* or cause and effect; as you sow so you reap. Each person has the liberty to enjoy the fruit of his/her fate, which is the result of his/her deeds whether in this life or a previous incarnation. There is no obligation to redistribute; there is no spontaneous method of trying to equalise. There is no conscience about someone being poor or miserable; for that is his bhagya based on his karma. Similarly, the poor may seek help but does not expect response as his right. He is basically reconciled that the cause of his problem lies in his own deeds earlier. If the rich Hindu is charitable, it is out of human sympathy or perhaps as a way of getting social acclaim but not as a matter of conscience or duty. So much for liberty!

When I decided to move to Delhi, Mirza said he would also move. For quite a while, I thought he was joking. In Calcutta, he lived in a flat with his siblings, on Congress Exhibition Road in Park Circus. Where would he reside in Delhi? With a journalist acquaintance who worked for *Qaumi Awaz* of the National Herald group. I needed to pay him only Rs 700 per month. This was early 1982 and I did not see how he could manage. Eventually he could not and did not. Before long, I had to find him a quarter with a helpful MP friend in Ferozeshah Road and then get him a job in the Congress office as an Urdu/English translator. Ahmed Patel, the present treasurer of the party, was very helpful. To begin with, Mirza and I were both freer in Delhi than even before. We had long chats. He was not curious to know anything about me except perhaps now and then about business. The questions were, therefore, almost all mine. And they became more candid as our acquaintance grew. Once, there was considerable controversy in the newspapers about fire crackers and sweets being distributed in the wake of a Pakistani victory in a cricket match against India. So, I asked Mirza point blank: why were so many Muslims in India pro-Pak? And as they were, why did they not migrate?

His reply in my words (his I have forgotten after these many years) was a counter question. Do you think that the *moortis* (idols) you bow before in the temple are gods? The answer evidently was no; the moorti is symbolic of an avatar of God or rather *Paramatma*. That means the moorti is God's proxy to enable the Hindu to focus his attention while worshipping. I could not dispute this contention. Well then for us Muslims, or at least some of us, Pakistan is a proxy for an Islamic state of our hearts' desire. Mirza continued by saying that even he felt glad when Pakistan won or gained something, but not necessarily at the cost of India. He claimed that the same Muslims celebrated a Pak victory, with equal zest, even if it was against the West Indies or Australia. Did not Hindu citizens of Britain applaud the Indian team playing against the MCC? The white British did not appear to object to the applause, he added.

What earthly use was Pakistan to the Indian Muslim? In

fact, the partition had put him to a disadvantage. Quite a part of the elite had migrated leaving behind the rest of the community. Moreover, together on the whole subcontinent, the Muslims were a much larger, more influential minority. In 1947, they were divided into two. In 1971, incidentally, they got trifurcated into three when Bangladesh seceded from Pakistan. Might be so, Mirza replied. But supposing two brothers find themselves surrounded, and only one can escape, should he not go? Or should they take the stand that either both go or neither? And for the chap who remains behind, there was the satisfaction that his brother had founded an Islam-e-Jamhuriya.

Such commitment, even when conflicting with one's own interest, to the brotherhood and to the idea of an Islamic state, seemed astonishing to a Hindu. I could not imagine that such altruism could be a reality. Especially when one considers that the sentiment was not confined to my Urdu teacher. It must be widespread; otherwise how could one explain the many Islamic triumphs? I am yet to meet a single Muslim who has admitted to me that Pakistan was a mistake. If self-interest was the consideration, there is no doubt that Partition divided the sub-continental *ummah* and thus left it weaker and the Indian section kind of orphaned. Evidently, the loyalty or the attachment to the dream of a Nizam-e-Mustafa even if in a different country, overrides an Indian Muslim's self-interest.

One winter morning Mirza came to the house as usual, but he looked angry if not also sullen. I happened to be free. I ordered tea which he had, probably felt better and became relaxed enough to speak up. I took him up to the first floor verandah where we could be by ourselves; so that he could unburden his anguish. One of his neighbours at Ferozeshah Road had annoyed him over a bucket of hot water. The neighbour happened to be an orthodox (bigoted according to my teacher) Hindu. The details of the incidence over, Mirza asked if he could tell me something frankly, to which I asked him to go ahead. 'Let me tell you quite frankly' Mirza began, 'that you Hindus just do not understand us Muslims. What is even sadder is that you have no interest in understanding us either. You hardly ever let us into your homes. You do not eat with us. You never listen to us. You educated Hindus pose as secular but stop short of any real interaction. Politicians flatter our leaders and coax us into voting for them. Behind our backs you hate us because you are mortally afraid of a bogey called the *mussalman*'.

'Do you know? We do not hate Hindus' he went on. 'We pity them because they are soft, self-centered and narrow-minded. It is for their good that we try to persuade them to also accept and become Muslim.' When I raised the question of forcible conversions, Mirza conceded that temptation of jobs and patronage might have been used to convert during medieval times but certainly no force. What about iconoclasts like Mahmud of Ghazni? To which his answer was he must have been substantively a robber and incidentally a Muslim. He destroyed idols in the temples, looted what was hidden below and went away. He did not stay back either to conquer, to rule or to convert Hindus to Islam. Did he?

How would Mirza explain the phenomenon of the Quwwat-e-Islam mosque near the Qutab Minar? A large part of it is built with stone pieces which evidently belonged to a Hindu temple. Why such desecration, insult and abuse? I asked. To which Mirza gave what to me then seemed a very interesting, although a bitterly ironic, explanation. How else could Muhammad Ghori announce to the people of Delhi that he had replaced the rajah as the sultan? Imagine the unavailability of most means of communication at the turn of the 12th-13th century. Replacing a popular temple with a mosque was about the only authoritatively telling way of doing it. Whenever and whoever came to pray at the temple from the surrounding or the distant places got the message with a bang. I read a similar explanation in a book about the time the Babri edifice at Ayodhya heated up as a controversy. But that was nearly a decade later.

According to Mirza, the desecration (he used the word demolition or replacement) of temples was almost entirely to do with power and little to do with religion. Only the popular prominent temples were affected. The peripheral ones were left alone because they were not so useful as media of communication. I was unhappy with this callous explanation and went on to try to corner my teacher's argumentation. What was Aurangzeb trying to announce when he desecrated several temples at Banaras, Mathura and other places? By then the Moghul dynasty had been well ensconced in power for a century and a half. Not only all India but the whole civilised world knew about it.

Aurangzeb was the only one among the Moghuls, and about the only one amongst all the sultans who sat on the throne of Delhi, who was at once a ruler and a missionary. He was a devout Muslim and dead against idol worship. He felt it was his mission to rescue the idol worshippers from heading for *jahannum* or hell, make them accept (*tasleem*) the final message of Allah as conveyed by his last prophet and thus give them an opportunity of going to *jannat* or paradise instead. His reintroduction of *jaziya* or a tax on *kaffir*s or infidels was another of his anxious ways of inducing Hindus to cross over to Islam. But even Aurangzeb did not use force, emphasised Mirza. Had he done so, the subcontinent could not have remained a Hindu majority area. Knowing the oppressions of the caste system, do you not agree that 75 per cent of the Hindus were sitting ducks for the arrows of Islamic proselytising? All the outcastes, then called Harijans, now Dalits, plus all the Shudras or once born, form the major portion of Hindu society. The twice born upper castes of Brahmins, Kshatriyas and Vaishyas comprise less than 25 per cent of all Hindus.

It was a long day interrupted only by lunch, tea and a few business telephone calls. My curiosity to know and understand more was whetted further but its satisfaction had to wait for another leisurely day when Mirza was worked up and I was relaxed. The suitable day took months to arrive, but it did on a Sunday when Nayana (my wife) was away in Bombay and neither Mirza nor I had anything else to attend to. We began at breakfast; the omlette put him in a good mood. The facilities for cooking meals were inadequate in his quarter at Ferozeshah Road.

I recalled how, several months ago he had accused Hindus of having no interest in understanding Muslims. I now wanted him to tell me what else I should know or understand since I was keenly interested. He began by swearing that a Muslim loved his land dearly, at least as dearly as a Hindu. Perhaps more because he expected to be buried in it; which means he expected to remain in his land longer than a Hindu who would be cremated into ash at death. And where he is buried is important to a Muslim. He would like to choose his grave if he could afford to do so. A little mischievously, I asked if he had any preference. Certainly, he retorted. If I were his true friend, and he died in Delhi, I ought to do my best to have him buried in the Baq-e-Billa *kabrastan*. Mirza's revered grandfather was buried there, and he wanted to be near him when he could.

As chance would have it, a couple of years later Mirza died of a severe heart attack in his dwelling. His job at the Congress Party office came in handy. Ahmed Patel, the general secretary of the party took special interest, and after considerable effort, a space was located only about ten feet from the grandfather's grave. The grave for Mirza was dug six feet deep very neatly; it took two men almost the whole day. Simultaneously, five about 3-cm thick slabs of red stone were cut, four for the four sides and one for the top. The floor of the grave was straight soil for the body to mingle with the earth. The digging over, the slabs were fitted. In a nearby masjid, the body was bathed, perfumed wrapped in a new white cloth and got ready for the final goodbye. At about 10 pm the maulvi read the prayers and the remains of Agha Iqbal Mirza were lowered. His younger brother and sister had come from Calcutta to be present. So were present to honour my departed Urdu teacher at the funeral Ahmed Patel and Jitendra Prasada, who was also treasurer and vice-president of the Congress party for some time. What Mirza had missed in life was made up by the glory of his funeral.

For me, the whole experience was an eye opener. I had never before imagined that a dead body is treated so well, even better than in life. I had seen, as a child, Christian funerals on Girgaum Road in Mumbai from the distance of my grandfather's verandah. The mourners dressed in their Sunday best. The coffin was immaculate and the body was dressed also in its Sunday best. A band played until the body was placed on the hearse. And so on. But it had not registered on me that all this ceremony signified the tribute that the near and dear ones paid to the person until his/her body finally departed literally for the lap of mother earth. The Muslim tribute was equally handsome as I saw it during Mirza's last journey.

I had been to two or three Hindu/Jain funerals. No dishonour is done to the body but ceremony is absent and there is a hurry to carry away and cremate the departed. This is perhaps appropriate in India's generally warm climate. If someone dies after sunrise, he/she should be cremated before the following sunset. And if death occurs after sunset, the funeral should take place before it rises again. But it is much more than the warm climate. It is the Hindu view that, once the soul or *jeevatma* leaves, the body becomes waste matter if not also a polluted mass which must be disposed off as promptly as possible. The belief in the transmigration makes the soul all important and the body no more significant than garments.

I recalled the sharpest illustration of this view which I had come across as a child of six or seven. Motilal Shroff, by then probably 75, lived with his joint family on the second floor of my grandfather's house. My cousins and I often wandered into Shroff's house to play with his grandchildren. I remembered I had once overheard the old man telling a visitor how he had been dropped to the floor on two occasions but had not died. Apparently, my mother had explained to me much later, some Vaishnav families put the dying person down on the floor, so that the death (the time the soul leaves the body) does not pollute the bedding!

In the Judaic or Muslim scheme of thinking there is only one life. There is therefore greater importance attached to it. By the same token, death has a finality. The best possible is, therefore, done for the body until it is to be returned to the earth. The soul then waits for *qayamat* or doomsday when God would decide who deserves to go to heaven or paradise and who should be consigned to hell or purgatory. This takes me back to which way our conversation went the day Mirza was angry. When would doomsday come, I asked.

Mirza answered that no one knows. But it should not be very long to go now. That was why Muhammad was the last prophet who had delivered God's final message. There was to be no further message or real change until doomsday. There was also no question of another prophet. There was simply no need.

Some time earlier, there had been tension in Pakistan over the Ahmediya sect which had been declared as non-Muslim. Mirza recalled this issue to illustrate his contention. This denomination was derecognised not for any doctrinal difference but because its founder Mirza Ghulam Ahmed had claimed to be a *paigambar* with a newer message of God. That was sacrilege for it contradicted the absolute Muslim belief that Mohammad was the last prophet. There were many Muslim sects that had differences with one another, continued Mirza.

The Sunni-Shia rivalry was legend but never has any Sunni (he was one) alleged that the Shias are not Muslim. Their faith in the message delivered by Prophet Muhammad was total. There could be no revision or amendment or a fresh message.

I was surprised. How would the faithful Muslims progress then? The world is changing more rapidly than ever before. How could a prescription, however perfect, given 1,400 years ago still hold good in absolute totality? Surely there has to be some revision, some adjustment? To this, Mirza responded with two simple points. For one, the message was not a human creation. It was divine, that of Allah. Two, it was comprehensive and eternal for it dealt with virtually all aspects of life forever. It was not confined to prayer, worship or ritual. The Holy Quran is not merely a religious text. It is a code of how to lead a good life perennially.

Would that not put Muslims to disadvantage? To the contrary, Mirza asserted. Is not the faith with which Muslims live and work unique? About the only comparable parallel could be the Jews. The Christians are so dispersed in their efforts. So much so that many a Protestant in Europe and America is supposed to have lost interest in Christianity, religion and God. He might have become a materialistic robot. The Roman Catholics were much more sensible, although the Pope should not have permitted the Reformation. That was the beginning of the Christian disintegration one witnesses now. Rebels like Calvin and Luther openly defied the Pope and yet they were not banned from calling themselves Christians. That was no way to run a faith. Another mistake might have been for the Pope not to assume temporal powers over Christendom. Had he done so, the gag of secularism might not have got going.

In Islam there was no such thing. At about this point, we were interrupted by someone or something, I cannot now remember. Pity indeed because my Urdu teacher had his views flowing fluently that day. So, we had to break up with a promise that we should resume the discussion before long. It took months before we could settle down to another leisurely chat. In the mean time we did talk on this subject. Often, I ran out of topics to use for practising my Urdu and hence what a Hindu should know about Islam according to Mirza kept bobbing up from time to time. What I record in the next paragraph onwards is the sum total of what I remember after well over a decade. Apart from the odd memory failure, there might be my faulty understanding of what Mirza said. And he was no great scholar; his views, therefore might not all be based on accurate knowledge. Nevertheless, what I am able to convey should broadly reflect the Muslim frame of reference.

Before narrating what Mirza called the gag of secularism, let me continue with the Muslim's love of his land into the bowels of which he literally goes soon after death. The Hindu impression is that the Muslim is usually not a nationalist, I posed. And anyone like Abul Kalam Azad who placed a priority on his country and its integrity had few Muslim followers. What did I mean by a *nationalist*? Someone who loved his country? If that be so, most Muslims were nationalist, Mirza asserted. Did he mean their first loyalty was to their country, I enquired. No; between country and religion, Islam usually commanded a priority. In fact, for a devout Muslim, his religion enjoyed his overriding priority. But so what? There is rarely absolute loyalty or love. Even a parent does not love his/her children equally. Are not there favourites and not so favoured?

Which Hindu could claim that his motherland is everything to him? Does even the most patriotic Hindu love his Hindustan more than his *family*? Would he rather die fighting than abandon his *matrubhoomi* forever if such a desperate dilemma confronted him? In any case, could I claim that all Hindus are nationalists or patriots? Must not there be quite a few potential Quislings, and many in-betweens? Nationalism is the political outgrowth of capitalism which is only about two centuries old in Europe. In India, it is hardly a century old. The Congress was founded in 1885. Human civilisation is 5,000 years old. Why did it make such a fetish of nationalism? Merely as a stick to beat the Muslims with?

In feudal times, the political loyalty was to the feudal master or lord; in tribal times to the tribe and so on. Muslims at least have been consistent for 1,400 years. For them, Islam is always above all. But being loyal to Islam does not mean being disloyal or against India. Was his argument then the same as that of the Jews, I enquired. That they were unnecessarily persecuted by the Nazis and the other anti-Semites? Mirza's reply was in the negative. The Jews have no mission. They do not try to convert non-Jews and bring them closer to God. The Muslims are at the opposite end in this regard. They do their best to bring as many non-believers into their fold as possible. They have a universal mission and are not self-centered.

Mirza often repeated that there should be justice towards all religions. I could not really figure out how he could defend, albeit half-heartedly, the re-imposition of *jaziya* by Aurangzeb and yet talk about justice. But I did not corner him on this contradiction for fear that he might close up and stop being candid. Moreover, my feeling was that he did not mean to support *jaziya*; he was so angry with his neighbour that day that he exaggerated a few of the points out of pique.

He was, however, consistently clear that secularism or the separation of the state from the church was un-Islamic. Prophet Muhammad was at once the spiritual and the temporal head of Islam. The *khalifa*s or the caliphs who followed him as his representatives were also popes and kings rolled into one. The Holy Quran was a spiritual as well as a temporal message. Secularism was a Christian and a European concept but a repudiation of Islam. There was no word or term in either Arabic or Urdu for the concept.

Paradoxically, Mirza was born, brought up and educated in Delhi, lived most of his life in Calcutta and returned to Delhi and yet could not entirely get Pakistan off his mind.

MUSLIMS, THEOLOGY AND DEMOCRACY

WHAT HAS happened in Turkey following the general elections held in June 2018 is the shift of the veto on national power from the army to the President. The change is not as revolutionary as is portrayed by some observers. It is true however, that Mustafa Kemal Pasha, the founder of modern Turkey after World War I did not have faith enough in his people to sustain Western-style democracy. He had, therefore set a tradition for the army to be strictly secular and to strictly monitor that country's government's distance from religion. It was made unconstitutional for a political party to have any religious leaning. Earlier, Kemal Pasha had abolished religious schools or madrasas as well as religious courts. He went to the extent of ending the Ottoman Sultanate as well as the caliphate of all Sunni Islam. In 1928, he further replaced the Arabic script with Roman letters for the Turkish language. Notwithstanding, Recep Tayyip Erdogan has replaced Turkey's parliamentary form of government with a presidential one. Will he go further towards one-man rule or stop here?

Our subcontinent has inherited a great deal of tradition from British rule. Mohammed Ali Jinnah was a constitutionalist; by temperament and training, he was an English-style lawyer but the Pakistan he founded could not sustain democracy. Bangladesh, most of whose people are less staunch as Muslim than Bengalis, also has a chequered record of democracy. Generals Zia-u-Rahman and Ershad and their tenures come immediately to mind: on the other hand, Pakistani history bristles with the dictatorships of Field Marshal Ayub Khan, Generals Zia-ul-Haq and Yahya Khan lasting almost three decades.

The Pakistani Constitution begins by assigning the country's sovereignty to almighty Allah alone and *not* to the people of Pakistan. It further asks the government to enable the citizens to order their lives in accordance with the teachings of Islam as set out in the Holy Quran and the Sunnah (practices of the Prophet). The Sharia is prescribed by the scriptures as law. It cannot be amended; what then would be the role of a legislator in a democracy? What kind of democracy does such a Constitution promise to promote? President Yahya Khan's regime in 1971 let the country break up rather than allow the clear majority leader, Sheikh Mujibur Rahman, become prime minister. Uncannily, the Bangladesh Constitution declares the state religion of the Republic to be Islam; that leaves not much scope for non-Muslims to progress as citizens with equal rights.

The Iranian national document declares that 'the society is based on Islamic principles which represent an honest aspiration of the Islamic Ummah'. There are frequent references to Quranic ordainments as well as repeated mentions of what

Imam Khomeini had said. The leadership of Iran should be in the hands of a holy person in order to prevent organs of the State deviating from their essential Islamic duties. Moreover, the army should be ideologically committed to fulfil the mission of jihad. Finally, the reader is reminded that the Iranian state is based on belief in one God. The Constitution is not the supreme arbiter of state affairs but the scriptures of Islam which all add up to non-democracy. Periodic elections merely help to choose governmental leaders.

The Constitution of Iraq more or less opens by declaring that Islam is the religion of the state. That of Kuwait begins swearing in the name of Allah the Beneficent, the Merciful. Saudi Arabia understandably has designed its green flag with these words in its centre: There is but one God and Mohammed is His Prophet. The last two countries have no pretensions to being democratic but at this rate, clearly they offer no scope for democracy.

The Holy Quran devotes a great deal of space on the evils of *kufr* or *kafir* societies and how to deal with them. Little wonder that wherever the old armies inspired by Hejaz (Mecca and Medina) conquered territories, those have almost comprehensively gone over to the Muslim faith. As Prof Bernard Lewis writes, it was a Muslim duty – collective in attack, individual in defense – to fight in the war against the unbelievers. In principle, this war was to continue until all mankind either embraced Islam or submitted to the authority of the Muslim state. Until this purpose was achieved there could theoretically be no peace.

India as a whole is about the only exception. Even then, if we add Pakistan and Bangladesh, we would be over 40 per cent Muslim. Admittedly, what is Bangladesh was converted largely by Arab traders and the *maulvis* (Islamic clergy) who accompanied them. Nevertheless, Pakistan and, to a little lesser extent, Bangladesh have also been intolerant in squeezing out most Hindus, Sikhs and Buddhists. The contrast has been India which has practiced toleration and, at the same time, run a successful democracy. This makes toleration a *sine qua non* of democracy; a proposition which applies to all real practitioners of this free system of government.

The root of intolerance is the innocent ambition expressed lucidly by the Prophet, quoted in the Hadith. His exhortation to his follows was 'marry women who will love their husbands and be very prolific, for I wish you to be more numerous than any other people' (*Miskatul Masabih* book XIII). More numerous than any other people – for all obedient Muslims this has meant that population increase is a top priority, whether by having more children or when possible by conversion. With this priority, coexistence is ideally not possible and, under compulsion, not welcome. The answer to avoiding compulsion or constraint on the free play of religious practice, another Islamic priority, is living in a Darul (land of) Islam. This priority sets off the propensity to separation in a Darul Harb (conflict). How can a *momin* (faithful) be happy living in a democracy? If he is stuck in say India, he merely makes the best of a no bargain.

In order to presumably keep Islam united, the powers that be in Hejaz, a thousand years ago or so banned *ijtehaad* or reinterpretation and insisted on *taqlid* or orthodoxy. This great step minimised clashes of opinions. As a contrast, Christianity happened to be more open-minded and, in the process, split into different denominations. The first bifurcation took place as early as in the 4th century when the Eastern Orthodox Church came up based in Constantinople. The 16th century witnessed a series of Protestant movements beginning with Martin Luther in Germany. By avoiding such splits, Islam has not allowed its practices to move with the progress of time. In the process, Muslims are out of step compared to other communities.

'Most of the now-advanced countries had developed institutions essential to the mass mobilisation of savings, the lengthening of individual planning horizons, and the exploitation of new technologies through structurally complex organisations. Therein lies a key reason why the Middle East fell behind in living standards and why it succumbed to foreign domination. As the institutional complex of the West gave rise to progressively more advanced commercial and financial institutions, that of the Middle East produced organisational stagnation within those sectors beyond direct state control. That equals 28 per cent of the average for high-income countries. Only three-quarters of the adults in the region are literate, as compared with near-complete literacy in advanced countries.' This is brought out in *The Long Divergence: How Islamic Law Held back the Middle East*, by Professor Timur Kuran.

Nevertheless, in some dominantly Muslim countries, there have been a few quiet changes. For instance, Tunisia abolished polygamy in 1957. After Partition, Pakistan has made divorce more difficult; taking on a second wife is also as difficult. But in India, being a Darul Harb, the clergy, wary of their followers being polluted by the secular environment, has enforced *taqlid* strictly and kept change at a distance.

WHITHER INDIAN MUSLIMS?

THOSE WHO remained in India after Partition believed that in the Indian Republic there was to be only one nation – the Indian nation – and no community could remain a separate entity on the basis of religion.

A group of Muslim leaders representing Uttar Pradesh, Bihar and Bombay, with anxiety written on their faces, called on Mohammed Ali Jinnah at Delhi's Imperial Hotel on the eve of his departure for Karachi in early August 1947. They asked the Qaid what is to happen to the ones being left behind. What was in store for them? He said they would have to look after themselves. They protested that they needed better protection and should not be left at the mercy of the Hindus. After all, they pointed out, it was because of them that Pakistan, the Muslim homeland, had been created.

Looking sternly at them, Jinnah said, 'You are mistaken; the whole world knows that it is I who singlehandedly brought

Pakistan into existence. I am its sole creator. No one else can take credit for it'. Replying to a similar question a few days earlier too, Jinnah had said that those left in India would have to look after themselves. He was not interested in their fate.

How ironical is it that it was the Muslims of Bombay, Uttar Pradesh and Bihar who were the first ones to respond to Jinnah's call for Partition and enthusiastically supported the movement for Pakistan. They became its vanguard. They were so fanatically charged by Jinnah's slogan of 'Islam in danger' and frightened by the bogey of Hindu domination constantly raised by him that they were easily misled. Even when Partition happened, they did not understand or pretended not to understand, they had wanted and helped create Pakistan, chosen Pakistan and it was their turn to leave. They failed to ask themselves how could the creation of a state in the faraway North-West – comprising of parts of Punjab, Sind, the Frontier and Baluchistan – and still further in the North-East, consisting of part of Bengal and Assam provide any security to the rest of the Muslims living in Hindu-dominated regions and spread over cities, towns and villages across the land.

Despite this, paradoxically, the Hindus and Sikhs have provided them with the warmth of security and more. In fact, the minorities, largely a euphemism for Muslims, enjoy greater privileges than the majority. Articles 25 to 30 of the Constitution of India are more than ample evidence of this. The Hindus have more than compensated the Muslims for the betrayal by their leaders. Yet, they protest against what they feel they do not have and entirely overlook the fact that their glass is more or less full.

Historian Francis Robinson had much to say about the Muslims in Hindu majority provinces, especially in Uttar Pradesh and their role in creating Darul Islam in the Indian sub-continent. A specimen, 'Uttar Pradesh Muslims were at the heart of Muslim separatism. They mainly founded and, with the exception of Bombay-based Jinnah, mainly led the organisation which represented Muslim interests in Indian politics. Syed Ahmed Khan founded in 1875 the Mohammedan Anglo-Oriental College at Aligarh, which directed early Muslim political activity and nurtured many Muslim League politicians'.

Syed Ahmed Khan followed this up with the establishment of the All-India Muslim Education Conference in 1886, which helped him impress his political will upon Indian Muslims. In 1906, large numbers of Muslims from UP flocked to Dacca to found the All-India Muslim League. In this organisation, the post of the secretary was the most powerful position; between 1906 and 1910 it was held by Muslims in Aligarh, and between 1910 and 1926 by Muslims in Lucknow.

After World War I, Muslims from the same provinces set up an association of the Indian *ulema* (Muslim clergy) and made the Central Khilafat Committee an organisation of all-India importance. The same Uttar Pradesh is still our largest State with the largest Muslim vote-bank. Indians need to look after it so that history does not repeat itself.

Moreover, Uttar Pradesh is the cultural home of subcontinental Muslims. Aligarh, along with its university, is the cradle of separatism and Jinnah was forthright enough to call it the 'arsenal of Pakistan'. More recently, we know that Deoband is the birthplace of the Taliban, the Islamic fundamentalist body which is wreaking havoc in Pakistan as well as Afghanistan. Students of the Aligarh Muslim University had campaigned in Punjab widely and vigorously for the League's cause for Partition in 1945.

When some Punjabis asked them, what was there in it for them as their province Uttar Pradesh would not be included in Pakistan, the reply reportedly was: For the service of Islam. Historian Venkat Dhulipala in his eminent work, *Creating a New Medina: State Power, Islam, and the Quest for Pakistan in Late Colonial North India,* has said that 'the new homeland was for setting up another Medina'.

British Prime Minister Clement Attlee sent a three-minister Cabinet Mission to India to work out a constitutional settlement for the Congress-League dispute in early 1946. Having heard out Jinnah, a member expressed anxiety at the huge number of Hindus remaining under Muslim rule if the demanded Pakistan were to come about. Jinnah's reply to this anxiety was that there will be many Muslims under Hindu rule in Hindustan. So, in case Pakistan misbehaves with the minority, Hindustan can do the same. But nothing of that sort happened; on the contrary, from 1948 onwards, Pakistan has almost rid itself of all its Hindus through religious cleansing.

As a result of the Muslim League's launching of the Great Calcutta Killings of August 1946, riots erupted in many places in the country. Jinnah used these disturbances as a reason for demanding a population transfer. In *The Transfer of Power 1942-47* edited by Penderel Moon, ICS, and others and published by the British Crown, Jinnah is quoted as saying, 'The exchange of populations will have to be considered seriously'. This shows that he was logical as well as pragmatic in his approach.

Prof M Mujeeb, former vice-chancellor of Jamia Millia Islamia, has commented that, 'if Mr Jinnah was sincere regarding Muslims as a separate nation and demanding a separate territory for them, it was his obvious and inescapable moral duty to define the boundaries of Pakistan, territorial as well as its citizenry'.

I reiterate that the only one who was quick to respond to Jinnah's Pakistan resolution of 1940 was BR Ambedkar, who published his *Thoughts of Pakistan* the same year (Thacker & Co., Bombay). He explicitly argued, 'Hindus have a difficult choice to make: To have a safe army or a safe border? Is it in their interests to insist that Muslim India remain part of India so that they may have a safe border, or is it in their interest to welcome its separation from India so that they may have a safe army? Which is then better for the Hindus? Should the Musalmans be outside and against or should they be inside and against? If the question is asked of any prudent man, there will be only one answer, namely, that if the Musalmans are to be against the Hindus, it is better that they should be outside and against, rather than inside and against. This is the only way of getting rid of Muslim preponderance in the Indian army'. No other Hindu was bold enough to even think through the far-reaching ramifications of Partition. Or prudent enough.

Constitutional expert Durga Das Basu, in his book *Introduction to the Constitution of India,* has commented, 'Muslims obtained the Partition of India on their own demand on the footing of the two-nation theory, and even after Partition, a section of the Muslim community preferred to remain in

India out of their own choice; nobody compelled them to remain in divided India'.When the Muslims opted to remain in divided India, they did not enter into any covenant with the government of divided India. No observation of Maulana Azad can be enforced as a legal covenant in any international court.

Basu went on to quote a 1955 apex court judgment, 'Those who preferred to remain in India after the Partition, fully knew that the Indian leaders did not believe in the two-nation or three-nation theory and that in the Indian Republic there was to be only one nation – the Indian Nation – and no community could claim to remain a separate entity on the basis of religion'.

All these efforts for Pakistan, the New Medina, were from eminent Muslims like Mohsin al-Mulk, Viqar ul-Mulk, the Ali brothers, Khaliq-uz-Zaman, Raja of Mahmudabad, Liaquat Khan, all from Uttar Pradesh, apart from Jinnah and Aga Khan who were from Bombay. In fact, if not for the Uttar Pradesh leaders, the League could not have been built nor would the Partition have been possible. What a paradox that 70 years on, not only Muslims of Uttar Pradesh but even those far south of the Vindhyas are demanding another Pakistan and India is not Hindu enough to provide the retort.

WANTING ANOTHER PAKISTAN

ASADUDDIN OWAISI has demanded to know the number of Muslims in the armed forces. Earlier he had asked for Darul Qazas (Sharia courts) in every district to be recognised by the government in India. Soon thereafter, the Deputy Grand Mufti of Srinagar, Nasir-ul-Islam, insisted on the same facility of Darul Qazas. He went on to say that if they were not granted, Muslims would be justified in asking for a separate homeland, which means another Pakistan. This has caused a great deal of apprehension in the rest of India.

When the Indian Penal Code and the Criminal Procedure Code were introduced in the 19th century, the British rulers had abolished the Qazas. A resurrection of these communal courts will damage the secular fabric of the country. Moreover, the Qazas tantamount to being Islamic enclaves within the Indian republic, a state within a state. In other words, India will become a half-sovereign state. However, in this era of vote-bank politics, is anyone listening?

The question of representation of respective communities in the armed forces was thoroughly examined by BR Ambedkar on the morrow of March 1940, when at Lahore the League passed the Pakistan Resolution. His findings and comments merit careful reading even today.

'Hindus have a difficult choice to make: to have a safe army or a safe border? Is it in their interest to insist that Muslim India should remain part of India so that they may have a safe border, or is it in their interest to welcome its separation from India so that they may have a safe army? Which is better for the Hindus? Should the Musalmans be without and against or should they be within and against? If the question is asked of any prudent man, there will be only one answer, namely, that if the Musalmans are to be against the Hindus, it is better that they should be without and against, rather than within and against. Indeed, it is a consummation devoutly to be wished that the Muslims should be without. That is the only way of getting rid of the Muslim preponderance in the Indian army.'

'How can it be brought about? Here again, there is only one way to bring it about and that is to support the scheme for creating Pakistan. Once Pakistan is created, Hindustan, having ample resources of men and money, can have an army which it can call its own and there will be nobody to dictate as to how it should be used and against whom it should be used. The defence of Hindustan, far from being weakened by the creation of Pakistan, will be infinitely improved by it. The Pakistan area, which is the main recruiting ground of the present Indian army, contributes very little to the central exchequer' (*Pakistan or The Partition of India*, reprinted by the Government of Maharashtra, 1990).

One of the committees appointed by former Prime Minister Manmohan Singh was that headed by Justice Rajinder Sachar; he had asked for the same information and the government was willing to provide it. But the chiefs of staff of the three services refused to do so, on grounds of national security. Even in the British era, once recruited, there was no counting as to who is a Hindu or Sikh or Muslim. How can sectarian soldiers fight in the face of the enemy? That tradition has been consistently sustained in the post-independent Indian armed forces.

It would be relevant to recall here that the Khilafat Committee formed on the morrow of World War I in 1919 and presided over by Mahatma Gandhi to save the Caliph on his throne endorsed that Muslim soldiers would not fight if India were invaded by a Muslim army, say from Afghanistan. The Muslim League headed by MA Jinnah endorsed this caveat. It is to the credit of our army after independence to have abolished such communal ideas. Does Owaisi, for his unsavoury political motives, want to reawaken the obsolete Khilafat sentiments?

Janaab Owaisi must appreciate that independent India has been large-hearted enough to accommodate his party founded by Kasim Rizvi and subsequently led by Abdul Rashid, the grandfather of Asaduddin. Their musclemen, who were thousands in number, were called Razakars. Their single point programme was to take Nizam's Hyderabad State into Pakistan. They failed to do so only because Sardar Vallabhbhai Patel had the will to send a force led by General JN Chaudhuri into Hyderabad. Little wonder the grandson, Asaduddin, would like to engineer another partition.

As for Mufti Nasir-ul-Islam's abominable demand for

another Pakistan, he needs to be reminded that India is yet to implement the logical corollaries of Partition that took place in 1947 – a Hindu India facing Muslim Pakistan. This is what Justice GD Khosla has recorded in his book, *The Stern Reckoning* (Oxford University Press). 'The Muslim League demand for Pakistan was based on the hypothesis that Hindus and Muslims constitute two separate nations, each entitled to a separate and exclusive homeland where they would be free to develop their culture, tradition, religion and polity. On any other ground, the partition of the country and the setting up of a separate independent State for the Muslims would have been indefensible. But the two-nation theory brought the problem of minorities into greater prominence than ever before, and partition, instead of offering a solution, made it even more difficult and more complicated. No matter where the line of demarcation was drawn, there would be Hindus, Muslims and Sikhs on either side of it, in a majority or in a substantial minority; and, whatever the geographical boundaries of Pakistan, large numbers of Hindus and Sikhs would, overnight become aliens and foreigners in their own homes.'

'Mr Jinnah made desperate efforts to evade the issue by promising protection and rights of citizenship to the minorities, but the nature of his demand was wholly inconsistent with these promises. How could millions of foreigners acquire rights of citizenship and equal status with the nationals of Pakistan; and if they could, why divide India – why not let Muslims continue as nationals of India? Mr Jinnah could find no answer to these questions and he was finally compelled to suggest an exchange of population. On November 25, 1946, Mr Jinnah, addressing a Press Conference at Karachi expressed the opinion that the authorities, both Central and Provincial, should take up immediately the question of exchange of population.'

For now, the Mufti deserves to be exiled and not allowed to return to India.

For Jinnah, along with his seven senior colleagues named Sir Feroz Khan Noon, Nawab of Mamdot, Mohammed Ismail, Pir Ilahi Bux II Chundrigar, Raja Ghazanfar Ali Khan and Ghulam Husain Hidayatullah wanted an exchange of populations. They were keen for all Muslims to migrate and gather in Pakistan and for all non-Muslims to go to Hindustan. They had all made public statements which appeared in the *Dawn* of 1946, a daily founded by Jinnah. In response to this proposal, Dr Rajendra Prasad, our first Rashtrapati for two terms, had suggested in his book *India Divided* that those Muslims who could not emigrate should be allowed to reside in India but as *aliens* with visas issued by New Delhi. Jinnah had agreed with this suggestion. What is tragic is that Pakistan did implement an envisaged exchange, but India did not.

Asaduddin Owaisi should realise that had Jawaharlal Nehru allowed this idea of exchange to be implemented, he would have either been a Pakistani or an alien in India without any voting rights. Let him, therefore, not be a party to generating communal tensions generally and in the armed forces particularly. Paradoxically, anti-India agitators like him are allowed to speak in public in India, against India. Try speaking against Pakistan in Pakistan.

FROM ALLAHABAD TO PRAYAG

DISCARDING PRAYAG and renaming the city Allahabad was a calculated insult to the Hindu faith, and to the sacred *triveni-sangam*. Ironically, this was done by one who has been promoted by Left historians as a super icon of secularism. That makes it not only ironical but also implies that virtually whatever a badshah, sultan or nawab did is secular unless proved otherwise. Using the name of the only God, the merciful and the beneficent, was Emperor Akbar's way of targeting the Hindu sacred with *his* holiest. What an extraordinary imagination by the founder of Din-e-Ilahi, the blend of all religions, the ultimate in the Indian version of secularism. Prayag becomes Ilahi-bad, now corrupted to Allahabad. Nowhere is Allah's name used for a city or street or shop.

As someone who believes in the European version of the separation of state and religion, the writer nevertheless feels that to involve Allah the merciful and the beneficent in such mundane matters as changing a city name is insulting God as he sees Him. Even the worst iconoclasts, who invaded India, do not appear to have committed such a heinous act. For example, Akbar's great grandson Aurangzeb did not go beyond ordering Islamabad for Mathura and Muhammadabad for Varanasi. How could Akbar, wise and very intelligent as he was, have resorted to involving Allah the omnipresent, the invisible apart from being beneficent and merciful, in the despicable deed of insulting people? Yet he did. All Yogi Adityanath* is doing in reverting to the name Prayagraj is to wash off the Mughal-e-Azam's unforgivable act of heaping humiliation on Hindus.

Akbar was as much an invader, after killing Hemu at the second battle of Panipat, as Robert Clive was after vanquishing Siraj-ud-daula at the battle of Plassey. The only difference was that Clive and his successors did not convert Hindus by force, whereas Akbar's successors did not hesitate to deploy the sword to open the Hindu's option to reach *jannat*. For being more ruthless, the Indian governments have honoured them by naming some of India's central streets of Delhi after them and are reluctant to make any changes thereafter. Similarly, dozen upon dozen cities and towns, not to speak of districts honour the invaders.

On the other hand, what the successors of Clive named after themselves such as Curzon Road et al have been renamed. Even the spellings of some indigenous names have been proudly altered such as Cawnpore into Kanpur. Bombay has

---

* Uttar Pradesh Chief Minister in 2018-19

become Mumbai, Calcutta Kolkata and Madras Chennai, all British given local names. However, Ahmedabad has not become Karnavati nor has Tughlak given Daulatabad reverted to Devagiri. But India's first political party and once an institution of secularism now feels outraged because Allahabad is standing up to shape the country's modern political history.

Muslims have mysteriously escaped the stamp of an invader in Hindu eyes. They have stayed in India for a thousand years; and 70 years ago, they took away a third of Hindustan and made it their homeland and called it Pakistan. On the other hand, the British ruled for 190 years, did not stay back nor did they take away any territory. Yet, they carry the stigma of an invader. Hindus pat themselves on their back for having waged a freedom struggle and sent back the British in 1947. Not a single street or city with a Muslim name whether Tughlaq, Lodhi or Babar has yet been replaced, except Aurangzeb Road in Delhi.

Muslim rulers exploited the land and its revenue to enjoy luxuries, ran harems, acquired jewels and build mausoleums. They hardly took any interest in promoting trade or industry and left no surplus for economic development. Their negligence caused India to miss the Industrial Revolution until after the British initiated modern mining, textile mills and other manufactures. Obviously, the British did so for profit but their ways of governance were such as to bring incidental benefits as well as modernisation to the country, be they the Railways, Post & Telegraph, the Laws, Universities et al. Moreover, the curiosity of British officers and scholars led to the discovery of what was ancient Indian civilisation which the Hindus themselves had largely forgotten. The Muslims destroyed more of the old, especially temples, and created very little new except their own mazhars and dargahs.

Agriculture was the main occupation but Muslim rulers ensured that the cultivators, who were 99 per cent Hindus, were left with no surplus. All kinds of taxes were used to extract as much state income as possible. The manner in which money was squeezed out of the cultivators has been described in a document of FerozTugluq's time and quoted in Vol. I of *The Cambridge Economic History of India*, 1982. It reads: 'A village was assigned to a trooper called Ziauddin, the sovereign having given him the right (haqq) over its poll tax (*jaziya*) and tax on cultivation (*ziraat*), so that he might spend the income on himself and his military equipment. The peasants, however, fled from the assigned village and settled in another village. Ziauddin insisted that the emigrants return to his village as it was his right to collect the poll tax from the peasants.'

A charge often levelled against the British is that they divided the Indians, that is, they sowed the seeds of discord between Hindus and Muslims in order to rule India. Was this largely true? Even after the British crown assumed direct rule in 1858, no attempt was made to divide the country again. Uncannily, the Viceroy for the princely states and the Governor General for British India were combined in the same person. Assuming that the British had adopted the policy of divide and rule, would they have taken the structural measures that they did early in their rule over India? For example, the three Presidencies of Bombay, Calcutta and Madras had been established independently of one another. Yet, they were brought under one umbrella by the Regulating Act of 1773.Thereafter, Warren Hastings was promoted from Governor of Bengal to Governor General of India. Decades later, the Agra Presidency was formed, also to be answerable to the Governor General.

If the policy was to divide, why was Lord Macaulay supported in his zeal for introducing English as the medium of instruction? This reform contributed more to bringing India together than any other. There was no *rashtrabhasha* (national language) then. And without education in English, would our leaders across the sub-continent have imbibed from the West the spirit of liberty and the concept of nationalism?

The British could have taken steps, with the full support of the princely rulers, to try to ensure that British India did not get easily integrated with the rest of the country. Instead, the Independence of India Act 1947, passed by Parliament in London, provided that every princely state must either join the Indian Union or the dominion of Pakistan.

The first gift of the English to India was the establishment of law and order across the country. Sir Percival Griffiths ICS, who served all his working life in India and wrote extensively, also deserves to be quoted. He was speaking at the City of London Tavern on the occasion of a dinner hosted for him. According to Sir Percival, on 6th July 1831, Raja Rammohan Roy said: 'Before the period in which India had become a tributary to Great Britain it was the scene of the most frequent and bloody conflicts. In the various provinces of the Dominion, nothing was to be seen but plunder and devastation; there was no security for property or for life, until, by the interference of this country, the great sources of discord were checked,

periodic riots with Hindus, so necessary for a Congress-style secular party to survive in power. Under communist secularism in Kerala and West Bengal, its rule was almost entirely riot free. So was the so-called Hindu rule under the BJP and earlier under the Jana Sangh in a couple of States; except for 2002 in Gujarat which were provoked by the burning of railway bogeys with 58 lives lost at Godhra. The lesson of this short history is that a Muslim minority can coexist with a Hindu majority. The reverse ratio, however, is not true as demonstrated by the rapid ethnic cleansing in 1947-48 in Pakistan and a similar but chronic process in Bangladesh.

The first lesson to be drawn from this paradox is that for Hindu-Muslim amity, the population of the latter community should not exceed 20 per cent. With 25 per cent in 1947, the Muslims were able to force Partition. This was despite being given reservations in jobs as well as separate electorates in 1909. Until 1940, they claimed to be a minority and then to justify Partition they changed to being a nation. In short, they have a chronic tendency to separatism.

Secondly, the ruling party should not come to power by playing the two communities against each other. The Congress had to remind the Muslims periodically what a riot is, and more of it would be their fate if they did not vote for the party. Otherwise, let the Muslim clergy hold a veto to power; for example, the Shah Bano case and government's rejection of court ruling, followed by the Muslim Women's Act.

The pinnacle of this Congress secret of success was reached in the ten-year prime ministership of Manmohan Singh who several times declared 'Muslims First' as his policy and also appointed five commissions and committees of whom the Sachar-led effort was the most talked-about. No wonder the five Modi-led years have been filled with complaints by Muslims and their friends that 'everyone' feels insecure. The Muslim clergy no longer holds the veto after 67 years of being used to it. That there has been virtually no rioting during the five years across the country is not appreciated.

Another feature of Muslim performance has been its failure to produce an eminent leader. Mohammed Ali Jinnah was the last one thrown up by the sub-continental *ummah*. Even he became prominent as a Muslim leader, as it were, more to fulfill the mass desire for delivering Partition and less as a community eminence.

A possible explanation could be that Islam as an ethos prefers autocracy, whether monarchical, military or civilian, but not Western type democracy. By contrast, in the subcontinent, the Hindu performance has been much better.

In the absence of responsible and respected leadership, the Muslim masses have been mesmerised by their clergy as well as the Congress. These two have worked in tandem; the only time the link had snapped was in the 1977, post-Emergency elections. Otherwise, their interests are similar. The former want to keep a grip on the followers while the latter need the votes. From its beginning the Congress has been pro-Muslim. For a glaring example, Gandhi had equated a hope for success in his 1921 Non-Cooperation Movement with a victory of his Khilafat movement to save the Caliph on the Turkish throne. The failure of both led to what Ambedkar called a 20-year Hindu-Muslim civil war until 1940, when the Pakistan resolution was passed at Lahore.

Almost a century later, Congress president Rahul Gandhi did not hesitate to admit that the Congress is a Muslim party. And why not? Because the grand old party has placed the community superiorly to the Hindus, especially when Articles 29 and 30 render Articles 14 and 15 a sham. Additionally, the wakfs, which own up to six lakh acres of urban land in the country, have been left untouched by the government, whereas the zamindaris and jagirdaris were abolished on the morrow of independence. These and other laws make Muslims appear to be the favourite offspring of India while the Hindus may feel like, as it were, stepchildren.

It is for the post-Congress governments, whether in the States or at the Centre to correct the misleading impression created on most of the Muslims. Citizens of all hues below about 45 years in age are mostly unaware of the facts of the Partition. Discussions in the media give the impression that free India's life began with the Constitution. The earlier years were all part of *jahiliya* or darkness.

An attempt should be made to inform people – who voted in which manner in the 1945-46 elections and the run up to Partition. As a backgrounder, how in 1940, the League declared that the Muslims were a nation and not a minority. It, therefore, had to have a separate homeland or Darul Islam. The League leaders wanted Muslims to transfer to Pakistan and all the rest to go to Hindustan. *Those who remained behind were to live as aliens with the help of visas issued by the respective governments.*

Instead, today Hindustan has probably more Muslims than any other country except Indonesia. The community itself claims to be poor and backward. It seems it appears to spread backwardness to the States it lives in. Today, the belt beginning with UP, and ending with Assam via Bihar and West Bengal is economically distinctly poorer than the rest of India. Although the Ganga flows across the belt, the soil is mostly fertile and there is a great deal of mineral wealth to mine, these States are poor. These States have to be pulled up and, more particularly, the Muslims.

If the writer were a Sunni Musalman, he would tell his people that not many of us can emigrate and therefore to live happily in India, we should join the mainstream. The licenced madarasas all over should be given say, four or five years, to come up in their standards to be affiliated to the mainstream boards like CBSE or ICSE. AMU and Jamia should cease to be Muslim or Islamia since they are entirely state-financed. If not a Uniform Common Code, the community itself could take the initiative and modernise the personal laws and draft a Muslim Code Bill.

All temples converted to mosques and which are readily re-convertible to mandirs should be vacated. Only 2,500 or so recycled (built anew with the debris of demolished temples) mosques may be left as they are.

All these suggestions would help the Muslims to integrate with the rest of the people of Hindustan and share the benefits of national prosperity. The Shias are already on the path to integration. Why not also the Sunnis?

All that is being recommended is to favour the ways of Dara Shikoh, away from the misguided whims of Aurangzeb. Both were full blood brothers. But the latter caused and presided over the fall of the Mughal Empire. Hindustan does not wish to fall similarly. Those who do not agree at all with the suggestions may consider Hijrat, also a recommendation of Islam.

Is it not paradoxical that an American professor should come to India to whitewash one of its diabolical emperors?

IS CONGRESS A MUSLIM PARTY?

WHILE HOSTING a number of Muslim intellectuals on 11 June 2018, Rahul Gandhi was reported by the Urdu journal *Inqilaab* to have stated, 'Yes, Congress is a Muslim Party'. This followed on the heels of the party's lending support to the setting up of Darul Qazas in every district as proposed by the All-India Muslim Personal Law Board. Earlier the Congress had refused to support the passage of the bill, already passed by the Lok Sabha, to prohibit instant triple *talaq*. The party leaders must have assessed that such support would upset many Muslim men.

'The provision of minority rights as enshrined in Articles 29 and 30 of the Constitution belongs to the same species. A full bench of the Supreme Court is currently hearing a case on this subject. It is to be hoped that the stand taken to begin with by Solicitor General Harish Salve, wherein those minority educational institutions, which receive special aid from the government, should cease to have reserved seats on religious lines, is accepted by the Supreme Court."*

It is not widely known that Articles 29 and 30 owe their origin to communalism. The Constituent Assembly was elected in January 1946. On 13 December of the same year, Jawaharlal Nehru, as the head of the interim government, moved, what was called an Objective Resolution, in order to appease the Muslim League, hoping it would not press for Partition. As it happened, the endeavour to appease the League failed and the country was divided.

It is useful to recall that the Constituent Assembly had been elected on the basis of Muslim constituencies – then called separate electorates – and 85 per cent of the voters had voted for the League whose single point manifesto then was Partition. Evidently, all the Muslims in the Assembly were beneficiaries of this 85 per cent vote.

What is extraordinary is that even after Partition, the Objective Resolution and the resulting articles continued to be debated as if nothing had happened on 15 August 1947.

In other words, what was proposed to placate the League and thereby avert Partition was enshrined in the Constitution *despite the creation of Pakistan.*

In the words of Jawaharlal Nehru, spoken in the Assembly on 8 November 1948, 'Nearly two years ago, we met in this hall and on that solemn occasion it was my high privilege to move a resolution which has come to be known as the Objective

---

* https://www.dailypioneer.com/2018/columnists/the-politics-of-appeasement.html

Resolution... It tried to embody the spirit that lay behind the Indian people at the time. It is difficult to maintain the spirit of a nation or a people at a high level all the time... Nevertheless, I hope that it is in that spirit that we have to approach the framing of this Constitution... always using that resolution as the yard measure with which to test every clause and phrase of this Constitution' (pages 317–318, *Constituent Assembly Debates,* Vol. VII 1999).

Articles 29 and 30 were described in the resolution as safeguards provided for minorities. In the process, considerable discrimination was introduced in the educational system. A school is either run by government or aided by state. In either case, the government has the final say in the policies of the school. If, however, a school happens to be run by members of a minority, the government does not interfere in its running. In effect, a school run by Hindus either accepts government aid and faces interference or abstains from the aid. Not so a school run by Muslims.

In spite of this background, the Constituent Assembly, on 9 November 1948, patiently heard ZH Lari, a Muslim Leaguer from UP who had got elected on a pro-Partition ticket. While pleading for reservation as well as special rights for Muslims, Lari said: We never said that Muslims in these parts are going to migrate to Pakistan. We are the children of the soil and as such we claim the rights of citizens of India.

Vishwambhar Dyal Tripathi, another member, shot back: 'What did your leaders do in Pakistan?' Prof KT Shah, yet another member, tried to insist that no expenditure on any private institution should be defrayed from the public purse.

Yet, Nehru and his government ignored the exhortations, and went on to enshrine in the Constitution financial burdens which most States are now finding difficult to bear. Let us consider this stark fact: the combination of a subsidy and freedom of management has led to proliferation of madarasas.

The Nehru regime was anxious to retrieve the mohajirs who had landed in Karachi. To take the example of Banaras weavers, Nehru's friend Sri Prakasa who was the High Commissioner said to them, "why have you come here? No one wants you here. Do get back home. Why do you want to destroy my city? It is you who have made it famous in the world." 'I immediately used to issue permits to them to go back', he wrote in his book *Pakistan: Birth and Early Days*.

Syama Prasad Mookerjee saw the riots in East Pakistan as part of a deliberate and cold-blooded plan to exterminate or expel the minorities from East Pakistan. It is this conviction which made Mookerjee suggest an exchange of populations. Nehru rejected this suggestion out of hand. As recorded in his *Selected Speeches*, he went on to explain: 'An exchange of population is something which we have opposed all along. It is something which I consider not only undesirable but also not feasible.'

In his book *Government from Inside*, Dr NV Gadgil, a senior member of the Nehru cabinet wrote: I have already described how systematically Pakistan drove out its Hindus and how they encouraged Bengali Muslims to enter and occupy some areas in Assam. The Indian government took no notice of these. On the other hand, Nehru was greatly annoyed when once Vallabhbhai suggested mutual exchange of Hindu and Muslim populations and a proportional division of land between India and Pakistan.

But one has to admit that such an exchange would have been beneficial in the long run. The Indian Muslim remained, on the whole, aloof from the mainstream of Indian life after Partition, but in almost all cities communal Muslim organisations continued their poisonous propaganda. Thousands of Muslims who had gone to Pakistan returned and were given back their properties. The Hindus received no such justice.

Indira Gandhi was comparatively less partial. Nevertheless, at the Simla Conference with Zulfikar Ali Bhutto, she let off 93,000 Pakistani prisoners of war scot-free although the Indian people were told that Prime Minister Bhutto had verbally promised to make the LOC in J&K the permanent frontier between the two countries, so that the Kashmir issue would be settled for all time.

Rajiv Gandhi was more confused but no less a player of communal politics. In 1981, the Madhya Pradesh High Court awarded an alimony to a long-divorced lady, Shah Bano. In 1985, a five judge bench of the Supreme Court dismissed her former husband's appeal and endorsed the alimony. However, the Prime Minister, exhorted by the Muslim clergy, nullified the Apex Court judgment by having the Muslim Women Act 1986 passed by the Parliament. Thus, the clergy was appeased but what about justice to a poor widow?

Sonia Gandhi has been consistently biased and her nominee Prime Minister, Manmohan Singh, not only appointed several committees for alleviating the Muslim community's socio-economic conditions and promising it the first 15 per cent of the country's resources. 'Muslims First' has been his oft-repeated slogan. To be fair to Rahul Gandhi, he is no more to blame than to say that he has been loyal to his long-set family and party legacy. It would also be pertinent to recall that Sir Syed Ahmed Khan, in his time, had advised Muslims to stay away from joining the Congress, because it was 'a Hindu party'. Qaid-e-Azam Jinnah believed and openly said that the Congress was a Hindu party. Yet, paradoxically, the party chiefs claim it is Muslim.

CONTRADICTIONS GALORE

BABRI DEMOLITION

I WAS at Ayodhya between 10.45 am and 5.45 pm on the fateful day of 6 December 1992. The whole township around the Babri edifice was chock-a-bloc with between two to three lakh people, most of whom had come from outside for *kar seva*. I spent the whole day on the terrace of a newish little building at a distance of what looked like a furlong from the edifice. Two of the domes were clearly visible; the third one was covered by tall trees from where I saw.

This terrace had all the VIPs on it. I dared not leave it to go down lest I be not readmitted. I had gone there with Keshubhai Patel and Sureshbhai Mehta who subsequently were successive chief ministers of Gujarat. In fact, I had gone on the request of Keshubhai, in our Contessa car. We spent the night of the 4th at Bareilly and that of the 5th at Lucknow. Next morning, it took us about an hour to drive past Faizabad to Ayodhya where we reached at 10.30. Fortunately, Keshubhai was recognised, as we got down from the car, by the karsevaks on duty. We were, therefore, respectfully conducted to the top of the VIP terrace.

The giving of short speeches, interspersed by the singing of devotional songs, was all that was happening until about noon. A microphone was on the terrace and a few of the VIPs took turns to address the mass of karsevaks. No doubt the atmosphere was charged with expectation but there was no apparent action. Then I saw youngsters climbing the domes and scratching them. In the course of the next hour, the surface of the domes became the colour of sand; it had been dirty black when we arrived in Ayodhya. While the youngsters on top were exhilarated, the crowd below uttered cries of thrill from time to time. For anyone who had the leisure to think, it was obvious that this was hardly the way to demolish a structure.

About this time two photographers ran to the terrace and complained that some five of them had been manhandled and the camera of one of them was snatched and smashed. I concluded: the target was not the photographers but the cameras, for the karsevaks inside the edifice were anxious not to be photographed. They were using crowbars to attack the walls where the dome began. This also I heard from the photographers as the terrace was too far to enable us to see for ourselves. Around 2.30 pm. I heard a dull thud followed by the crowd sighing with delight. This was presumably the collapse of the dome that was not visible from the terrace.

The chanting of bhajans and the shouting of slogans continued with the help of the mike on the terrace which was full of not only the VIPs but also many a police officer. There were many policemen in uniform at Ayodhya. They, however, had little to do since the karsevaks on duty were making sure that there was no disorder. In fact, the only incident of manhandling of a person during the whole day was that concerning the photographers. One could now see a stream of young karsevaks bringing away small pieces of debris to take home as souvenirs.

Then suddenly, at 3.40 pm, one of the two remaining domes collapsed followed by clapping this time. Cries of delight could be heard as there was mass clapping. The scene on the terrace had to be seen to be believed. The jubilation was uncontrolled, and more tears of joy were shed at Ayodhya that day than probably on any another occasion in the history of mankind. At 4.30 pm fell the thin dome and for a while the birth town of Lord Rama saw a riot of exhilaration. Over the centuries thousands of temples had been desecrated across north India. At last the Hindus felt that they had got back at least one.

As the sun was receding on the short winter day, it was getting cold and the karsevaks began to melt away from the Ramjanmabhoomi. We left the terrace at 5.30 pm and were back in our cars before 6 pm. Soon after, we heard on the radio that Kalyan Singh had resigned and subsequently his ministry had been dismissed.

On our way back to Lucknow, many scenes kept coming to my mind. The one scene that kept coming back the most was that of the huge edifice, tall and with thick walls standing without the domes. At the little motel in Lucknow, probably at 9.30 or 10.00 pm, we heard Prime Minister Narasimha Rao speaking on television. He condemned the demolition as a dirty shameful act and promised to rebuild what he called the Babri masjid. I, therefore, wondered before falling asleep whether the central government would replace the three domes post haste. The whole of next day was spent in returning to Delhi.

I recollect I had caught a nasty cold. Yet I wrote a letter to *The Pioneer* which I personally delivered at its office in Bahadurshah Zafar Marg. It was published the next morning, on 9 December with the headline, 'There have been darker days'. On the 10th morning, most of the newspapers had a photograph of a small flat little temple with a tiny flag flying on its centre. This was the little temple quickly built by the central government on the site of the demolished edifice for the Ram Lalla idol which, incidentally, I had the privilege to see on the terrace on the 6th evening. A pujari had brought there the black idol, in his anxiety to save it from the crash of the descending domes.

Seeing the photograph of the new Ram Lalla temple, I realised that the Rao government had demolished the walls of the edifice. I was thunderstruck by the hypocrisy of the secular Government of India which had promised to rebuild the masjid. It had, instead, demolished its walls all in a matter of 60 hours between the evening of the 6th and the morning of the 9th when this photograph must have been taken. No picture of the edifice sans its domes has been seen by anyone I know. Evidently, Ayodhya was cordoned off while the walls were demolished, and its debris removed with extraordinary dispatch.

I said to myself – even if I could not help a friend rebuild his broken roof, at least I would not go to his house and demolish his walls. But that is what happened at Ayodhya in December

1992. I have published several letters to this effect but little notice seems to have been taken of them. Only when former Home Secretary Madhav Godbole blamed Prime Minister Narasimha Rao, there appeared to be excitement.

Paradoxically, a Congress PM and a BJP CM appeared to have combined to demolish an unwanted structure.

SHIAS VACATE RAMAJANMABHOOMI

WITH THE skies darkening with terrorism, it is time that India encouraged its Shia citizens, more so after their warm gesture on Ayodhya. The country would benefit by offering a balance between the Shias and the Sunnis.

The Uttar Pradesh Shia Waqf Board's suggestion to the Supreme Court that the erstwhile disputed Babri mosque site at Ayodhya was the 'most revered place of birth of Maryada Purushottam Sri Ram' is yet another signal – a reminder that the Shias of India do not wish to be mixed up with the aggarandising Sunnis. They are different, with a distinct perception of Hindustan and their commitment to the country.

That the Shias are not only distinct and nurse antagonism towards the Sunnis is well-known for centuries. In the Hindu view, the difference got blurred possibly due to Aga Khan, who led the All-India Muslim League in the beginning of the 20th century and Muhammed All Jinnah as the final creator of

Pakistan. Jawaharlal Nehru's biased policies for the Muslims, euphemistically called the minority, and his inclusion of Articles 25 to 30 into the Constitution to ensure minority rights, further confused the Hindus into lumping all the Muslims together.

An advanced nail in the coffin was hammered by former Prime Minister Manmohan Singh when he repeatedly declared 'Muslim first' and promised them the first claim to the country's resources. At the same time, the Shias did little to distance themselves from the Sunnis in the Hindu eyes, partly because their leaders felt that they would not carry credibility because Jinnah was still a reminder of separation in the memory of the Hindus. Every time they saw a Pakistani President addressing on television, Jinnah's portrait was prominent as the green flag. And the Qaid (leader) was as Shia as he could be. To begin with, he was an Ismaili Khoja, some of whose womenfolk still perform Swami Narayana *puja* at home.

If India was always a pluralistic society, why did the partition take place? Evidently, there were recent Aurangzebs who demanded partition and divided the country.

Born of the same father and mother, Dara Shikoh was a truer embodiment of India's ethos. The national goal must be to induce as many Muslims as possible to adopt the example set by Dara Shikoh and move away from his younger brother's worldview. India has given a hospitable shelter to everyone who came here. Would that have been possible if Indians were bigoted? On the other hand, look around the world and see how Europe and America are finding it difficult to welcome refugees and migrants.

This writer had years ago met an Abbasbhai Rambhai in his shop in Panaji. Except for scholars and the interested, few Hindus are aware that the Shias and the Sunnis fell apart during the same 7th century era when Islam was born. The belief is that Husayn ibn Ali was an outstanding person and deserved to succeed his father, Ali ibn Abi Talib, the fourth Caliph who was murdered in 661 AD. There were those who felt that ideally the Caliphate should belong to Prophet Muhammad's bloodline. Husayn ibn Ali was his nephew and son-in-law, and was known as a Shia. Instead, old man Muawiyah I became the fifth Caliph who in turn ensured that his son Yazid would succeed him. Husayn ibn Ali was denied the privilege which angered the followers of Husayn ibn Ali and his successors.

The animosity climaxed into the Battle of Karbala, some 80 kilometres from Baghdad where Husayn ibn Ali, his brother Hasan and their male sons and followers were killed. The enmity grew with time. In India, Sunni-Shia riots during the Muharram month were an annual feature in Lucknow until a few years ago. Shia Islam is the official religion of Iran and nearly all its people. Saudi Arabia represents the opposite pole of Islam, namely the majority Sunni faith. The world's Sunnis regarded the Caliph as spiritual as well as temporal head of Islam until Mustafa Kemal Atatúrk of Turkey abolished the institution in 1924 and exiled its head, the entire Ottoman family from Istanbul.

The Shias did not follow the Caliphate and did not harbour any transnational loyalty. Uncannily, if one watches an India-Pakistan cricket match with a group of Muslims, those who applaud Indian batsmen scoring boundaries are mostly Shias. With the skies darkening with terrorism, it is time India encouraged its Shia citizens, more so after their warm, welcoming attitude on Ayodhya. The intensifying antagonism against Shias in Pakistan and scattered sentiments that this minority be ostracised out of Islam should widen the intra-Islamic gulf in India. The civil war in Syria has not helped matters either. The governments and the people of both Pakistan and Bangladesh will remain dominantly Sunni.

India will benefit by offering a balance between the two sections. Another sector which is beginning to cry out for help are the women. We cannot be satisfied with a court striking down the triple *talaq, nikah* and *halala*. Polygamy could be more difficult to abolish in India as it is prescribed in the scriptures. A Uniform Civil Code is likely to find communal resistance. But the proposal to legislate a Muslim Code Bill parallel to the Hindu Code Bill should find wide support among the women of minority communities. With women released from the potentially constant threat of unilateral divorce, men as well as the entire community is likely to undergo a revolution.

Hopefully, the Shias will continue to give a lead to social reform. They should be complemented for having come a long way already from the time a Shia had led the carving out of Pakistan. Paradoxically, in India, the Sunni voice has been heard for the last 75 years, rather than the friendly Shias.

RETURN KRISHNA JANMABHOOMI AND GYAN VAPI

SEVERAL OPPOSITION leaders have objected to a resort to Parliament if the courts are unable to decide soon on the issue of the site for the Ramjanmabhoomi Mandir. The Muslim leaders are not magnanimous enough not to quibble about the site as a land issue. It is a much greater issue of 'faith' in which most Hindus solemnly believe that Rama was born there. Fair enough; as a believer in national amity, the writer would look for a prompter alternative. Neither the Krishnajanmabhoomi in Mathura nor the Gyan Vapi mosque next to the Kashi Viswanath temple in Varanasi suffers from any such obstacle. The *idgah* built over the Krishnajanma site is an ordinary structure, which came into being in Aurangzeb's reign, and is used by a few namazis on Fridays. Underneath the mound, whereupon existed the Krishna mandir, is now the janmabhoomi *dera* which is as modest a structure as a garage.

In his *Mathura: A District Memoir*, FS Growse of the

Bengal Civil Service has recorded his exhaustive survey and research about Brajbhoomi. He was so overwhelmed by the vandalism that visited the area repeatedly, that he wrote feelingly, although his home was in far away England. To quote: thanks to Muhammadan intolerance, there is not a single building of any antiquity either in the city itself or its environs. Its most famous temple – that dedicated to Kesava Deva (Krishna) was destroyed in 1669, the eleventh year of the reign of the iconoclast Aurangzeb. The *idgah* erected on its ruins is a building of little architectural value.

Mahmud Ghazni was, however, the first iconoclast to vandalise Mathura. That was in 1017 AD, about which Growse wrote: If anyone wished to construct a building equal to it, he would not be able to do so without expending a hundred million dinars, and the work would occupy two hundred years, even though the most able and experienced workmen were employed. Orders were given that all the temples should be burnt with naphtha and fire and levelled to the ground. The city was given up to plunder for twenty days. Among the spoils are said to have been five great idols of pure gold with eyes of rubies and adornments of other precious stones, together with a vast number of smaller silver images, which, when broken up, formed a load for more than a hundred camels. The total value of the spoils had been estimated at three million of rupees; while the number of Hindus carried away into captivity exceeded 5,000.

To go back to Aurangzeb, over two centuries after the desecration, Growse felt that of all the sacred places in India, none enjoys a greater popularity than the capital of Braj, the holy city of Mathura. For nine months in the year, festival follows upon festival in rapid succession and the *ghats* and the temples are daily thronged with new troops of way-worn pilgrims. So great is the sanctity of the spot that its panegyrists do not hesitate to declare that a single day spent at Mathura is more meritorious than a lifetime passed at Benaras. All this celebrity is due to the fact of its being the birthplace of the demi-god Krishna.

Today Balkrishna is worshipped in a little room which appears like a servant quarter attached to the back of the idgah. Pathos can be experienced by any visitor, whether a devotee or otherwise. To paraphrase William Shakespeare, not all the scents of Arabia would suffice to wash away the sins of Ghazni and Alamgir at Mathura. And since it is not possible to claim back what was destroyed long ago, the return of the idgah and the *shuddhi* of Krishnajanmabhoomi or the birth place of Krishna, is the only alternative.

Coming to Varanasi and the Kashi Vishweshwar temple, for the sake of impartiality, it is best to again rely on an Englishman, Reverend Mathew Atmore Sherring of the London Missionary Society who resided mainly at the holy city between 1852 and 1880. He toured the whole area repeatedly and surveyed the scene from a religious point of view.

In his book *Benares: The Sacred City of the Hindus*, Sherring referred to Al-Beruni who is one of the important sources of Indian history. He came to India with Mahmud Ghazni who reached as far as Benaras during his ninth incursion into India. Some decades later, Muhammad Ghori, after defeating the Kannaujian monarch, Jaichand, marched to Benaras where he was reported to have destroyed many Hindu temples. Thereafter came Aurangzeb who changed the name of the city to Muhammadabad.

The temple of Vishweshwar was systematically demolished by him. The large collection of deities stored on a platform called the court of Mahadev, in the northern side of the temple, were found from the debris. As recorded by Sherring, extensive remains of this ancient temple were still visible, and they formed a large portion of the western wall of the mosque which was built upon its site by the bigoted oppressor. Evidently, the former temple was much larger than the present one, which is really small for so important a shrine. But there was a reason for it. The new temple was built at the behest of Rani Ahilyabai Holkar long after Aurangzeb's desecration. Sherring explained that, the demolition of temples was not inspired merely by a hatred for idolatry or by greed for loot. It was also driven by a desire to humiliate the Hindus. How does one explain that the masjid built by Aurangzeb had to be bang next to the Gyan Vapi or the well of knowledge?

The mosque built by Aurungzeb on the foundations of the old or original Vishweshwar temple of lofty appearance, is of interest, not for its own sake – being a structure without any striking beauty in its own right – but on account of the ancient remains with which it is associated and from the materials of which it has largely been constructed.

The mosque is altogether composed of the remains of an ancient temple, of large dimensions and of very elaborate workmanship. The high pillars, moreover, on its northern face have been transferred from the same spacious building. These remains are Hindu; and it is unquestionable that the edifice, which was destroyed in order to make way for 'the mosque, was an old temple of Vishweshwar. An excellent ground-plan of this temple, prepared 'from minute examination of the extant remains'; it was drawn by James Prinsep, and published by him, in his *Views of Benares*.

There is no doubt, in our mind, that the Vishweshwar temple stood on this site, and was destroyed by the Mohammedans, who, as usual, transferred its stones to their own mosque. Between the mosque and the temple of Vishweshwar is the famous well, known as Gyán Vāpī or Gyān Kūp, well of knowledge, in which, as the Hindus believe, Bhagwan Shiva resides.

What greater evidence is necessary for the government to not exercise its sovereignty and take over these edifices which were parts of invaders' loot? Not doing so would be tantamount to an act of omission committed by a half sovereign power. It is clear in terms of statesmanship that the Muslim leaders should give up the temples at Mathura and Benaras and the government should receive them.

An interesting reverse example of wise politics was displayed by the Punjab Premier in 1938, Sir Sikandar Hayat Khan at Lahore. The High Court gave a verdict that the Shaheedgunge Gurdwara should remain with the Sikhs although it had once been a mosque. The Muslim League wanted the Hayat Khan government to appeal to the Privy Council. But he rejected the idea on the ground that by the same logic the Muslims would have to give up hundreds of mosques and dargahs, including Ajmer Sharif. So, it was best to let the principle of adverse possession prevail. Regrettably, after Partition, there was no such wisdom and the Gurdwara was violently taken over by the Muslims.

Paradoxically, Shaheedgunge was in a Muslim-majority province and yet the Sikhs obtained their gurudwara. Mathura and Benaras are in a Hindu majority country, after having sacrificed one-third of its land area to Pakistan. Yet two of our holiest temples have not yet been returned to us.

NATIONALISE WAKFS

EVER SINCE the institution of *wakf* was established in Arabia in 1185 AD, no attempt has been made to curb its adverse effects. On the contrary, the law was made more favourable for the stakeholders, especially in far away India even while wakf was abolished by many middle-eastern counties.

Whether the Uttar Pradesh government can reclaim properties which stood on agricultural land or transfer them as wakf assets by holders having no ownership is a topical question. It appears that the Allahabad High Court had asked the government to reclaim them. However, the apex court has, on appeal, stayed the judgment. It would, therefore, be interesting as well as relevant to know how the institution of wakf was established in India.

The Muslim strategy, ardently supported by self-styled secularists, is to insist that the Babri Masjid is a disputed property which is best adjudged by a court of law. Since in

India justice is invariably delayed, the hope is that no decision is likely to be made in the foreseeable future. Thereafter, the scope for an appeal is enormous. To play on the soft sentiments of most Hindus may not be difficult, especially on the plea that a property when turned into a wakf goes into the ownership of Allah, the merciful.

The wakfs are the biggest urban landlords in India. Their origin dates back to the life and times of Prophet Muhammad. The institution began with a place called Khaybar in Arabia. It was a genius model of acquisition for turning a conquered property into an inalienable ownership. So is written by Asaf AA Fyzee in his book, *Outlines of Muhammadan Law*, Oxford University Press (OUP), Delhi, 1999.

Joseph Schacht, an international authority on Islamic law, in his book, originally published by OUP in 1964, said, 'The Wakf has one of its roots in the contributions to the holy wars which Muhammad had incessantly demanded from his followers in Medina'. For one thing, a wakf property is an outcome of conquest. If any further proof of expropriation is required in this context, the temple-turned-mosque provides it. The corollary to this premise is that the conflict over the temple should extend to question the validity of the institution of wakf itself.

Uncannily, none other than the Caliph of all Sunni Islam and the Ottoman emperor, Mehmed VI, thought it fit to abolish the institution in his empire in 1917. Thus, there are no wakfs in Turkey, Libya, Egypt, Sudan, Lebanon, Syria, Jordan and Iraq. In 1956, on the morrow of Tunisian independence, President Habib Bourguiba also abolished wakfs.

Although every *wakif* or donor claims that he has handed over the property to Allah, the merciful, Muslim leaders, ranging from the conservative Caliph to the modern Bourguiba, did not think so. Fyzee goes on to observe that the importance of the institution will be better understood if we take into consideration the enormous extent of wakf land or the possessions of the Dead Hand in the various countries of Islam.

In the Turkey of 1925, three-fourth of the arable land, valued at then 50,000,000 Turkish pounds, was endowed as Wakf. At the end of the 19th century, one half of the cultivable land in Algiers was dedicated. Similarly, in Tunis, one-third; and in Egypt one-eighth of the cultivated soil was 'in the ownership of God'. But it was already realised by the beginning of the 20th century, first by France and later in Turkey and Egypt, that the possession of the Dead Hand spelled ruin. The institution of wakf was in some respects a handicap to the natural growth and development of a healthy national economy.

In 1830, the French government took over the *habous* or wakf in Algiers, and later on in Morocco. Elsewhere, government control was made more stringent. In 1924, the Turkish republic abolished the Ministry of wakfs and it was taken over by a general directory, or by the secular state administration, as we would call it. In Egypt, it was Mohammad Ali who first confiscated all agricultural wakfs and compensated the beneficiaries and in 1924, the Wakf Ministry came directly under the control of Parliament. Although in Russia, wakfs existed in Muslim districts for centuries, soon after the revolution such endowments were confiscated and declared state property.

The religious motive of wakf is the origin of the legal fiction that wakf property belongs to God; the economic ruin that it brings about is indicated by the significant phrase: The Dead Hand. Wakf, to some extent, ameliorates poverty but it has a dark side too. When a father provides a certain income to his children and descendants, the impulse to seek education and the initiative to improve their lot gradually decreases. Charitable aid often keeps people away from industry, and lethargy breeds degeneration. Furthermore, some people, who desire fame by making endowments, obtain property by shady means, amounting to exploitation. Land deteriorates in the course of time; no one is concerned with keeping it in good trim; the yield lessens.

In India, instances of mismanagement of wakfs; of the ineffectiveness of *mutawallis* (managers); and of the destruction of wakf property have often come before the courts. For India, there are several other arguments that support the abolition of wakfs.

The dispute over a wakf in the late 19th century eventually went up to the highest court of colonial appeal, namely the Privy Council in London. The four British judges described the wakf as 'a perpetuity of the worst and the most pernicious kind' and declared it to be invalid. In the Privy Council, the judges were Lord Watson, Lord Hobhouse, Lord Shand and Sir Richard Couch.

A gift may be illusory whether from its small amount or from the uncertainty. If a man were to settle a crore of rupees and provide ten rupees for the poor, that would be at once recognised as *illusory*. It is equally illusory to make a provision for the poor under which they are not entitled to receive a rupee till after the total extinction of a family; possibly not for hundreds of years; possibly not until the property has vanished away under the wasting agencies of litigation or malfeasance or misfortune; certainly not as long as there exists on earth one of those objects whom the donors really cared to maintain in a high position. Their Lordships agreed that *the poor have been put into this settlement merely to give it a colour of piety*; and so to legalise arrangements meant to serve for the aggrandisement of a family.

Fyzee has deeply regretted that the Privy Council judgment did not prevail in India. The Mussalman Wakf Validating Act, 1913, proved to be the saviour of this institution. No attempt has since been made in India to either abolish or curb the adverse effects of wakf. On the contrary, the law was made more favourable to the Muslims as a result of the Act of 1995. To quote Fyzee: Speaking for myself, and in the light of actual experience, it is unfortunate that the opinion of Lord Hobhouse in Abul Fata's case did not prevail in India.

Wakfs in India date back almost to the beginning of the Sultanate of Delhi. S Athar Husain and S Khalid Rashid, in their work, *Wakf Laws and Administration in India*, Eastern Book Company, Lucknow, 1968, have traced their history. According to them, Sultan Muizuddin Sam Ghaor dedicated two villages in favour of the Jama Masjid of Multan and handed its administration to Shaikhul Islam, the *imam* of the mosque.

Another commentator, Ahmedullah Khan has recalled several properties that were brought under wakf much earlier, like the *dargah* of Moinuddin Chishti at Ajmer Sharief as well as Nagaur in Rajputana, Hansi and Ajodhan in Punjab, the Dargaḥ-i-Sabiri at Kalyar and the dargah of Shaykh Ahmed Abdal Haqq at Rudauli.

The government of independent India found it expedient not to interfere with the operation of the wakf laws. Political expediency dictated this unfortunate approach just as Article 44 of the Constitution – with regard to the personal law of the Muslims – has remained a pious lip-service. Paradoxically, on the morrow of independence, *zamindaris* and *jagirdaris* were abolished as were the princely States and merged with the rest of the country but not thc wakfs.

AKBAR AND AURANGZEB

THERE IS little doubt that Akbar has gone down in history as a grand strategist of statesmanship, especially vis-à-vis his vassals and people. He sat on the throne of Agra at an early age of less than fourteen, soon after winning the Second Battle of Panipat, defeating and killing Raja Hemachandra Vikramaditya. Unlike many a sultan, evidently Akbar must have sat back and thought that he had to portray an image of not being seen as anti-Hindu and certainly not a kafir hater, as most Muslim rulers were. This is not to say that Mohammad Jalaluddin Akbar was not a Muslim at heart. He certainly was, as evidenced by his naming his new religion as Din-e-Ilahi which meant 'Religion in praise of Allah'. He did not pretend to have seen any new vision, lest he is rejected by the Islamic clergy. To be doubly sure, by using the word 'Ilahi', which meant 'in praise of Allah', he remained safely on Islam's side. This pretention ensured that all the Muslim courtiers and support would remain with him and hopefully faithful to him.

Unlike his predecessors, Akbar did not invade the territories of rajas in northern India. He merely sent emissaries to propose to them alliances with the Mughal court. As far as possible, he did not disposes the Hindu rulers of either their land or wealth, or their titles. He merely expected them to fight for the new confederation as and when required as well as send an annual tribute as it were, for the defence of the confederacy, as and when needed. It would appear that the Akbarian alliances were a prototype of British Lord Richard Wellesley's subsidiary alliances, although Akbar was far more subtle and did not station Mughal troops in the rajas' territories. In the bargain, he commanded respect rather than resentment. The rajas felt quite honoured to be present at Akbar's court rather than feel humbled. In no way did Akbar carry Islam on his sleeve and on all social occasions, it was ensured that the atmosphere would be secular, if at all, somewhat more Hindu than Muslim.

Despite all these measures, the one and only Maharana Pratap could not be persuaded, nay deceived. He refused to play Akabar's game and fought against the latter till the last breath of his life. What is uncanny is that other Hindu princes learnt nothing from the Maharana's example nor understand even a hint of the imperial deception that was being served by Agra. Nevertheless, Akbar must go down as a rare bloodless conqueror of empire. The myth of Akbar being a secularist, incidentally, well ahead of his time, flourishes till this day.

Had Aurangzeb learnt any lesson from his great grandfather, India might have been another Indonesia – Islamic all the way, and yet painting the walls of its buildings with the image of epics Ramayana and the Mahabharata and naming its first president Mohammed Sukarno (Su-Karna, straight from the *Mahabharata*; the first son of Kunti and the elder brother of Yudhishthira), and naming a subsequent president Megawati Sukarnoputri. But heavens willed Indian destiny otherwise.

Akbar built an empire whereas Aurangzeb took on himself the honour of designing its disintegration. He had no strategy, no deception and no game plan, except to subdue more and more territory. His obsession for land went to the extent of abandoning his resplendent capital Delhi and expending more than half his career in the Deccan alone. It almost goes to the credit of Akbarian consolidation that no part of north India threatened to secede from the Mughal Empire, while Aurangzeb fiddled on the hills of Deccan. His pastime was to demolish temples, be they at Mathura, Banaras, Somnath and a hundred others. He could not suffer to see a torch burning in Vrindavan and hence surgically cut the Gobind Dev Temple into half. He then had a *mehrab* constructed on the new lower roof of the mandir, so that he could pray on the roof of his surgery. This is the most original achievement of Aurangzeb in the course of his half-century reign. No preceding sultan or subsequent ruler has performed such an architectural surgery. Although, over the centuries, iconoclasts have rained hammers upon some 3,000 temples.

To the Hindu, a mandir is a divine residence, rather like what Bethlehem is to a Christian. It is not just a prayer hall or a roof over the mehrab in a masjid to guide the namazi in the direction of Mecca. The Sultans saw the idol or the 'but' as un-divine. If that be so, why does a Christian church have a crucifix and a Catholic one, also the statue of Virgin Mary?

Why a mehrab, why in a masjid except to focus the attention of the namazi towards Allah? Surely, if this was not so, a mere hint of a hilal or crescent would be sufficient to show whither Mecca.

There is little doubt that Aurangzeb suffered from acute sadism. Or else, how does one explain the bricking up alive of two sons of Guru Gobind Singh and earlier the beheading of Guru Tegh Bahadur? The Sikhs were not the only people whom the emperor went after with a vengeance. It was the same story with the Jats centered around Bharatpur. The Rajputs were driven to open negotiations for an alliance with the Marathas. The saga of Marathas starting with Shivaji is well known. One by one, Aurangzeb made enemies and embittered them. He hurt so many, but by doing so, he also awakened the non-Muslims to the oppression and cruelties of an Islamic state. How poles apart Akbar and Aurangzeb were. Paradoxically, the deceiver and his subterfuge is hailed, the one who is straightforward a believer is condemned.

JINNAH AND GANDHI

MOHAMMED ALI Jinnah for years was popularly known as the ambassador of Hindu-Muslim unity; this was a compliment paid to him by Gopalkrishna Gokhale. That was not surprising, as at the age of 16 he had left for London to matriculate and join the Lincoln's Inn to become a barrister-at-law. From known accounts, he had no contact with religion. His extra-curricular interests were visits to the Parliament at Westminster and going to hear random speeches by mostly unknown men called soapbox speakers at Hyde Park.

He returned to Bombay and the first proper assignment he got was as a temporary Presidency magistrate, which by the very nature of its function, was one of impartiality between the litigants. Subsequently when Jinnah switched to advocacy at the High Court, most of the solicitors who sent him clients were either Hindus or Parsis. The majority of his clients were Hindu because they comprised the business community.

Socially, he found himself most comfortable with Parsis. Having spent his formative years in London, he was also at home with Englishmen. He made several Hindu friends like Kanji Dwarkadas and Diwan Chaman Lall.

What he considered fair he supported, whether in public or in the Viceroy's Legislative Council, to which he reached at in an early age. For example, he had the law making wakfs illegal reversed with retrospective effect. On the other hand, he did not support the Khilafat movement and criticised Gandhi's presiding over it as the Sultan of Turkey was no concern of India's.

As for politics, in the words of his biographer Hector Bolitho, 'his first aim was the Indian National Congress'. Religion did not get a chance to enter his bloodstream. He did not go to masjids to pray nor did he learn to say namaz. According to his younger brother Ahmed Ali, who was a friend of the writer's grandfather Dharamdas Vora, neither he nor Mohammed Ali acquired *pyjamas* for performing namaz. Little wonder that Jinnah was unpleasantly surprised when in 1915, Gandhi said in his speech at Tejpal Hall that he feels honoured especially because he has been welcomed by a *Mohammedan* leader. Jinnah had presided over the welcome reception organised after the Gandhis had finally returned from South Africa to Bombay.

Before long, seeds of disillusionment had been sown with Gandhi's street or mass politics as well as what Jinnah considered the former's indifference to communal politics. Gandhi's hobnobbing with Mohammed Ali and Shaukat Ali who were orthodox Musalmans all the way created further rift. Jinnah disapproved of the Non-Cooperation Movement of 1919, which Gandhi had to withdraw in 1921 because of the violence at Chauri Chaura. What was worse was the Mahtama's equating the freedom of India with success of the Khilafat movement.

Jinnah's final disillusionment with the Congress had to wait until 1928, before then he could not think of his politics without the Congress. His first biographer Hector Bolitho quoted him, 'my sole object is to serve the cause of the country as best I can'. His faith in Hindu-Muslim unity did not weaken, in spite of the terrible evidence that the differences between the two communities were so deep-rooted that no politician could ever hope to dispel them.

In 1946, the British ministers' Cabinet Mission asked Jinnah: 'Do you realise that the Pakistan you are demanding will leave substantial Hindus under Muslim domination?' Jinnah replied: 'That will be so; but I will leave many more Muslims under Hindu domination in Hindustan.' Surprised at this reply the Mission said: 'How does it then resolve Hindu-Muslim discord? It will only perpetuate the hostilities.' Jinnah persisted: 'I will free at least two-third Muslims from Hindu domination.' Jinnah was no visionary although he was integrity personified to his clients, he was a brilliant advocate and at his peak was considered the highest paid lawyer in the British Empire. It is fair to presume that he meant to be equally loyal to his followers who comprised most of the Muslims of the subcontinent. The only unanswered question was whether his loyalty superseded his ego which, according to his brother Ahmed Ali, insisted that he should be *numero uno* (number one) wherever he happened to be.

He was aware that the partition also meant the division of the Indian ummah (including the Shias of whom he was one). In February 1948, for the first time, he visited Dacca (now Dhaka) and also addressed the university students. In the course of his speech, he declared that Urdu would be the sole national language of Pakistan. Evidently, he had no clue to the local sentiments which preferred their language to their religion, if and when the chips were down.

Thus, the seed for the secession of East Pakistan had been sown, a tree which took 23 years to grow fully. That made it the trifurcation of the ummah. Had this not happened, an undivided India would by now be 40 per cent Muslim. With tactical voting, the country would have a Muslim prime minister. Hindu culture would have been emaciated if not also eliminated. After all, there are only three per cent minorities left in Pakistan and a mere eight per cent Hindus remain in Bangladesh. Thus, in the end, Jinnah unwittingly happened to work to enable Hindu civilisation to be what it is today; vibrant and not kaput.

Gandhi was in most ways the opposite of Jinnah. Except that their families hailed from towns in Saurashtra, Gujarat not far from each other. Jinnah's origins were at Dhoraji while Gandhi was from Porbandar. They both matriculated in London and became barristers-at-law. Neither pursued any academics further. Jinnah proceeded to be an outstanding advocate whereas Gandhi could not do well in the courtroom. He had read the Bible but apparently he had taken no trouble to understand Islam. Yet he firmly believed that only if there was Hindu Muslim unity, the British could not rule India for long and would have to leave their empire. Right through his career, on return from South Africa, he appeased Muslims so that they would be on his side, no matter what the sacrifice by Hindus. One can only wonder at this obsession.

One guess is that he felt the British had humiliated him for no rhyme or reason. Soon after his return from England to Rajkot, his brother Laxmidas was involved in a matter of missing royal jewels. Prince Bhavsinh was probably the culprit but Gandhiji's brother was accused of being an accessory after the mishap. The issue was in the hands of the British agent Oliphant whom Gandhi knew as they had incidentally met in London and had had a friendly chat. Gandhi went to call on the agent to seek his sympathy for Laxmidas. But for Oliphant, the matter was official and no one should influence his opinion outside. Gandhi, however, was persistent and did not give up despite a clear exhortation by the agent. Eventually, the peon was asked to throw out the visitor. The incident became the talk of the town as Gandhi was a local man, hence it was very shameful for him. Another humiliation he suffered is well known and that was at Pietermaritzburg station where he was thrown out of the first class compartment because he was dark skinned. The colour discrimination was quite rampant there.

On the morrow of World War I in 1919, Sunnis in India were agitated over the threat from the victorious allies, to the Sultan of Turkey, to his throne as well as to his Caliphate or Khalifat. A committee was formed to pressurise the British not to remove the sultan. Gandhi promptly agreed to be the president of the committee. What business had a Hindu to be involved with the Caliphate? Jinnah kept away from the movement but Gandhi saw a chance to endear himself to the Muslims.

The issue, known in India as the 'Khilafat' issue, was not clearly understood by the masses who vaguely perceived it as 'Islam in danger'; before long the Moplas of the Malabar coast went wild by looting, raping, butchering and converting Hindus. It was an almighty holocaust; many leaders including Annie Besant, ex-President of the Congress, Sir Sankaran Nair and others condemned the tragedy. Gandhi's only comment was that the Moplas were 'obeying the tenets of their religion'.

When in 1924 Hindus were massacred in Kohat, Gandhi commented to the effect that Muslims were friends while the Hindus were cowards. In 1939, across Shikarpur in Sukkur district of Sindh province, took place a nasty riot. In Gandhi's view, the Muslims were brave enough to defend themselves whereas the Hindus lacked strength and bravery. Earlier in 1926, one Abdul Rashid murdered Swami Shradhananda, successor of Swami Dayananda Saraswati, in his sickbed. The Congress Party collected funds for the defence of Rashid and deputed one of its leaders and a leading advocate to save him. The court sentenced him to death by hanging and yet some 50,000 co-religionists attended his funeral. Gandhi's comment was 'I have called Abdul Rashid a brother'.

Despite all this pampering of Muslims, Gandhi gained hardly any following or even influence over members of the community. At the 1931 Round Table Conference in London, he took, from the British Prime Minister Ramsay MacDonald one week to achieve Hindu, Muslim and Christian unity. He failed to do so and openly apologised. The result was the 1932 Communal Award given by Ramsay Macdonald, which conceded the Muslim demands.

In many ways, Gandhi imagined to be what he wished. When asked about the cause of the communal divide, he blandly replied that riots were coeval with British rule. Once it ended, they will disappear! Ambedkar had commented that between 1920 and 1940, there was an intermittent civil war; he meant between Hindus and Muslims.

In 1940, on the morrow of the League's Pakistan Resolution, Gandhi had said of partition: 'over my dead body'. Yet some days later, according writer DG Tendulkar (quoted by Mushirul Hasan in his *India's Partition*) the Mahatma observed that the Muslims must have the right of self-determination. We are at present a joint family, any member may claim a division. In September 1944, he met Jinnah at his Malabar Hill residence continually for 15 days. At the end they agreed on every point; except that Jinnah insisted on partition before freedom, whereas Gandhi wanted freedom first and then partition.

When in 1946 and early 1947, the Muslim League kept asking for an exchange of populations, Gandhi turned a stone deaf ear. In January 1948, a couple of days before he was assassinated, Syama Prasad Mookerjee, accompanied by Rajkumari Amrit Kaur, had rushed to plead with Gandhi to agree to the League proposal of an exchange of populations. The reason for the desperation was the flood of refugees coming in from East Pakistan into West Bengal. The Mahtama's response was that the partition was a territorial, not a communal, division. Such was his self-delusion.

As part of the partition exercise, 55 crore rupees were due to be paid by New Delhi to Karachi. Before the sum could be remitted, marauders called *mujahidin* from Pakistan had perpetrated the unfortunate mayhem on the hapless Kashmir Valley. The Indian army had to go to its help, leading the two countries into a state of war. The Nehru/Patel government thought that was hardly the time to make payments to an enemy. But Gandhi, who had neither protested nor fasted when Partition was announced in June 1947, now insisted that Karachi be at once paid the 55 crore and resorted to a fast unto death in order to coerce New Delhi. Willy-nilly, the payment was made.

VP Menon, who acted as the right hand man of Sardar Patel for the integration of princely States, concluded in his book called *Transfer of Power in India* very interestingly. He wrote Gandhiji particularly emphasised that the minorities were a sacred trust in the hands of the majority. In short, Gandhi lived for Muslims and eventually died for them. Gandhi and Jinnah were two of the last century's most paradoxical giants. Jinnah helped create Hindu India, Gandhi died for the Muslim.

SUBHAS BOSE MADE THE BRITISH DEPART

MOHANDAS GANDHI and Subhas Bose were a remarkable paradox. Their goal was the same: freedom from British rule. They were some 30 years apart in age which should have distanced the chances of a clash. Gandhi hailed from Gujarat, whereas Bose was a son of Bengal. Both had studied in England, which should have made communication between them on the same wavelength. On his return from Cambridge, the first thing that Bose did was to call on Gandhi at Mani Bhawan in Bombay. Having paid his respects, the young man expressed his desire to join the Congress and work for freedom. This was in July 1921, the very day he had reached Bombay.

Bose then proceeded to Calcutta and soon began making a name for himself in Bengal as a potential national leader. On the other hand, Gandhi was soon up to neck in his brand of activities. After the defeat of his country in World War I, the Sultan of Turkey felt threatened with his dethronement and exile imminent as well as the possibility of being removed from his position as the Caliph of all Sunni Islam the world over. Under the leadership of Maulanas Muhammed Ali and Shaukat Ali, Indian Muslims agitated for saving the Caliphate. Seeing an opportunity for endearing himself with the Muslim masses, Gandhi also took up the cause and even became the president of the Khilafat Movement Committee. For getting Hindu sympathy, if not also support, the Maulanas welcomed Gandhi's elevation in 1919. Mohammed Ali Jinnah saw the movement as being of no concern to Indians and did not get involved.

The tragedy at Jallianwala Bagh took place in April 1919. It so happened that in 1920, Gandhi launched his non-violent Non-Cooperation movement as his first massive step for throwing out the British from India. The package was called Swaraj by him and Gandhi linked it with Khilafat.

His was to be a four-stage struggle against the British government. First, all honors and titles, all medals and dignities conferred by the British were to be surrendered. This was a harmless gesture, merely the *hors d'oeuvres* before the full dinner. The second step was to ask all lawyers to suspend their practices, all government officials to leave their offices, and all parents to recall their children from government supported schools and colleges. The third step was to call upon the soldiers to lay down their arms. The fourth step was to bring about a massive refusal to pay taxes. For his own reasons, based more on ignorance of Islam and less on knowledge, he believed that provided there was Hindu-Muslim unity, the challenge could be overcome. This explained the somewhat ludicrous sight of a Hindu presiding over a purely foreign Muslim affair, namely the Khilafat movement.

The year 1921 saw unfolding of a number of violent incidents, especially in Bombay which Gandhi was there to witness personally. He was shaken but carried on with his Non-cooperation struggle. In February 1922, a police station in Chauri Chaura was set on fire and many a constable was killed. The incident shook many, including Gandhi, who reacted by calling off the Non-cooperation movement. A few months earlier, the Moplahs of Kerala who were upset with the British government and also disappointed with the progress of the Khilafat movement, resorted to an unprecedented genocide of Hindus across the Malabar coast. Maulana Hasrat Mohani commented: everything is fair in love and war. Gandhi empathised with him and wrote that there is no greater nationalist nor a greater lover of Hindu-Muslim unity than the Maulana. So obsessed was the Mahtama with Hindu-Muslim unity which was, he felt, the secret weapon for booting the British out of India. Unfortunately for Gandhi as well as the Sunni Mussalmans, the Khilafat movement went up in holy smoke when by 1924 Mustafa Kemal Pasha abolished the Caliphate and exiled the Sultan of Turkey for good.

When he found time in between his programmes, Gandhi propagated the charkha and khadi spun on it. They were to help the farmer to earn some extra rupees when he was not occupied tilling the farm. Khadi was not only anti poverty but also a symbol of economic liberty which swaraj was meant to bring with it. The rich were asked to take to wearing only khadi in order to patronise the poor spinners and weavers. Soon he began to be called the Mahtama and every Indian came to know about him. The crowds he attracted at his meetings were unprecedented. So were his prayer meetings and the *bhajans* which were sung at them became widely popular. The message of freedom to the masses had been delivered at a speed and in a manner which only Gandhi could have.

Remember there was no radio until 1927 and it belonged to the British as well. Nevertheless, the progress towards freedom was made at London's pace and not at Gandhi's or at his Congress party's. The Viceroys, the governors and their officers knew how to handle Gandhi's whimsical ways and his peaceful tactics. At most, the police had to use lathis, tear gas and only when isolated did the men have to fire bullets. The Mahtama, they flattered, by jailing comfortably and at times luxuriously in the Aga Khan Palace or at Birla House. The equation was cordial and the style of mutual treatment congenial although freedom remained distant. Hindus and Muslims remained as inimical as ever, not to talk of unity or even indifference. In Ambedkar's view an intermittent civil war raged between the two communities for 20 years, 1920 to 1940.

Regardless of whether Gandhi was in jail, hospital or quietly praying in his ashram, mysteriously, people, especially the Hindu masses could not forget him. No great political activity took place between 1922 when the Non-cooperation movement was called off and the Dandi march to produce and sell salt without paying tax. It appeared to have been conceived out of Gandhi's impatience at nothing happening. Several hundred volunteers and sympathisers marched with their leader from the Kochrab Ashram in Ahmedabad to the sea side of Dandi, a village in south Gujarat. While it aroused publicity, it was no startling event although the police beat up some 300 who were caught making salt. They were hospitalised but the tax on salt was not withdrawn. It was another thorn of failure in Gandhi's cap of achievement except that he did manage to keep the lamp of the needed freedom alight.

A parliamentary commission was appointed by Westminster under an MP, John Simon, to suggest ways and means of associating more Indians for the governance of the Crown's brightest jewel. The Report was useful for drafting the Government of Indian Act of 1935 which in turn was used as the skeleton for writing the Indian Constitution. The Indians however, whether the Congress or the Muslim League, did not cooperate with the Commission as no Indian had been co-opted on the commission. Instead Gandhi ordered the Congress to resort to Civil Disobedience which did not go far. Again, the propaganda value of this movement was enormous, its constitutional dividend was nil.

The Congress abstained from participating in the first Round Table Conference in 1930 but did send Gandhi as its soul representative to the second in 1931. The conferences had been called by Prime Minister Ramsay MacDonald of Great Britain. The most ticklish issue was severe disagreement between the Hindus and the Muslims. Gandhi, in his wisdom, volunteered to resolve the centre of the logjam within a week. He failed and had to openly confess his failure. The 1932 conference was not attended by the Congress and otherwise nothing was achieved. The Prime Minister saw no alternative to making the famous Communal Award whereby the Muslims were given what they wanted. Yet Gandhi continued to enjoy the glory of a mahatma.

In 1939, Germany attacked its neighbour Poland. Britain and France, as per their given guarantee, declared war on Germany. World War II had thus commenced. British colonies were not consulted but this issue did not come to a head until the Japanese in December 1941 attacked the American naval base at Pearl Harbour in the Pacific Oceans. When the war spread to Asia, the Congress felt it had a right to be consulted. In protest, its provincial ministries under the Government of India, 1935 resigned. Soon thereafter, on 8 August 1942, the Congress held a meeting at Gowalia Tank park and passed its Quit India Resolution under Gandhi's stewardship. The leaders were promptly arrested and stayed in jail for some two years, meanwhile leaving most of the political space in the country to Jinnah and his League. That proved a mistake.

On the morrow of the Pakistan Resolution being passed by the League in March 1940, Gandhi had reacted by declaring: partition over my dead body. By September 1944, he had become anxious enough on the issue that for a fortnight, he met Jinnah for 15 days to resolve the question. The discussion between the two leaders have been published by the English journalist Michael Nicholson.

In 1946 Jinnah and the League lost their patience and decided to show the Congress that the Hindus and Muslims could not coexist in the same country any more. They also considered it important to let the British realise that the country had to be divided soon as its two communal components could not live together amicably. They declared 16 August 1946 as a Direct Action Day to be inaugurated in Calcutta. Thus, over the next several days took place the notorious Great Calcutta

Killing which in turn led to more and more riots across north India.

Then on, it was onwards to the 3 June 1947 declaration by Viceroy Lord Mountbatten about the British decision to hand over Pakistan to the League at Karachi on 14 August 1947 and India to the Congress on the following day. Thus, it was Jinnah who won on his point: division before freedom. Gandhi could not even clinch his preference for Independence first.

Remarkably, Gandhi did not have his way on any issue since he took up Non-cooperation and also the Khilafat movement in 1919/20 through his career as the supremo of the Congress until his assassination on 30 January 1948. He failed with every initiative, whether against the British or with regard to friendship with the Muslims and together throwing out the British. Yet with every failure, Gandhi was glorified more and more by most Hindus.

Subhash's performances were excellent as well as successful in the 16 years of the time he joined the Congress. Before the end of 1937 he was elected president of the Indian National Congress. Over the years it was clear to Gandhi that the man believed that the end justifies the means. This was in contrast to the Mahtama's commitment to non-violence whether the end is achieved or not.

In March 1913, Subhash Chandra Bose matriculated with flying colours; he stood second in the entire Calcutta University. Soon he joined the Presidency College for a BA degree in philosophy. Early in 1916 there occurred a commotion at the college. A Professor Oaten had reportedly man handled some students; a few days later he again beat a student. The students were angry and a small group thrashed the professor. Somehow Bose was identified as the most guilty and was suspended; as a follow up he was expelled from the college. He had to miss a year; the following year he managed to get admitted to the Scottish Church College, also a prestigious institution. Probably as an effect of World War I, a India Defence Force, rather like today's National Cadet Corp, had been started. Bose joined and enjoyed this brush with military training, especially rifle shooting.

In that very September, Bose's father offered to send him to study at the University of Cambridge and simultaneously appear in the Indian Civil Service (ICS) examination. He was evidently a natural student and stood fourth in entire ICS test. He also did well at the final examination at the university. In July 1921 he returned to India. The same day, the 21st at Bombay, he called on Gandhi who happened to be in station. They had a happy meeting. Back in Calcutta, Bose joined the Congress Party, having earlier resigned from the ICS.

As described by Prof Sugata Bose in his biography, *His Majesty's Opponent*, in February 1938, Subhas Bose arrived in Haripura, near Bardoli in Gujarat; to preside over the Congress. His chariot was drawn by 51 oxen indicating the warmth of his welcome in Gandhi's home province. Both the leaders were warm and cordial although there was a difference in ideology between them. Bose believed on the lines of Sri Aurobindo that the righteousness of the saint's holiness must be complemented by the warrior's sword. Violence cannot be eschewed on grounds of political morality although it can be kept aside as a strategic or a tactical expediency. Gandhi, on the other hand, preached non-violence as more essential than defeat or victory in the struggle for freedom from British rule.

Additionally, Bose was known to be a leftist among Congressmen whereas Gandhi held his old views such as the economy to be based on the village. The leftists were influenced by the industrial West as well the then more recent Soviet communist ideas such as national planning. Nevertheless, despite his differences with the Congress right wingers, Bose had a successful innings as president in 1938. In his travels through the provinces as well as from the pulse of many a Congressman, he got the feeling that he was popular. And he deserved another innings as president in 1939.

On the other hand, the right wingers like say Sardar Patel and Abul Kalam Azad found Bose too aggressive and radical. Moreover, KM Munshi reported that he was in touch with some Germans, undesirable at the time. To be overtly anti-British internationally was not liked in the Congress. By January 1939, the controversy over the 1939 presidentship turned acrimonious. Pattabhai Sitaramayya became the right wing favourite; yet Subhas Bose did not withdraw and forced an open election, which he won.

Gandhi took his candidate's defeat as a personal discomfiture. He and all his supporters ensured that president Bose could not form a Working Committee. He realised that he could lead the Congress only with the cooperation of its high command and saw wisdom in his resigning. He saw no point in splitting the party. Instead, he formed a Forward Bloc within the Congress.

When the gathering clouds of crises burst into rain in Europe during May-June 1939, Bose stood out as His Majesty's

Opponent while the other Congress leaders did not wish to embarrass the British Crown. To quote from his biography, 'no compromise with British imperialism: this was Bose's theme and motto during 1940'. On 2 July, he was arrested under the Defence of India Rules. Before long, he went on a hunger strike in the Presidency Jail in protest against his arrest without his having done any wrong. For fear he might die, the authorities transferred him to his Elgin Road house as under house arrest. A ring of security was thrown around his house.

The enemy's enemy was one's friend. On this military logic, Subhas decided to get out of India and go to Germany, which was at war with Britain from May 1940, first in France. Sitting in Calcutta, or for that matter anywhere in India, he was not going to be able do anything significant for the freedom of India.

With the help of his nephew Sisir (son of elder brother Sarat Bose), he soon began planning his escape incognito from India by the land route. He was first driven to Gomoh railway station for an onward journey to Peshawar and then to Kabul. He was then helped by the local diplomats of Italy, Germany and Russia, which were all allies at the time in 1940-41. As Orlando Mazzotta, with an Italian passport, Bose proceeded to Moscow via Samarkand. By 2 April 1941, he reached Berlin where he was allotted the garden house of a previous foreign ambassador in a near suburb of the German capital.

He broadcast regularly to people from the German radio. But other than that, he had to kick his heels for two years in Berlin. On 29 May 1942, he was able to meet Adolf Hitler who was sympathetic to sending Bose to Japan where he could be more useful to the cause of the Indian freedom. But it took up to 9 February 1943 for Bose and his assistant Hasan to sail in a German submarine towards the Indian Ocean. About 400 nautical miles from Madagascar, they were transferred from the German vessel to a Japanese submarine which had come all the way from Penang in Malaya especially for Bose. In all, it was a three month voyage by submarine. Indeed a unique adventure!

From Penang, Bose flew in a Japanese plane to Singapore on 2 July 1943. There were two to three million Indian civilians in Southeast Asia which provided a large enough base for Subhas' struggle for freedom. On the basis of Asia for Asiatics, the Japanese had told the captured British Indian soldiers that they had no intention to hold them as prisoners of war. But, on the contrary, help them to flight the British for the freedom of their country.

Between forty to fifty thousand Indian soldiers were ready to quit the British masters and fight for freedom. This is how the Indian National Army, INA or Azad Hind Fauj took birth at Singapore in 1942, as it were, in anticipation of Netaji Subhas taking over its leadership. Bose met the Japanese prime minister Hideki Tojo in June 1943. Thereafter, the arrangement of alliance was officially finalised.

Just remember that most of the recruits were not only trained, battle hardened soldiers but also those who had broken the vow of loyalty they had sworn to the British Crown. This was a key development, that love for the motherland superseded the sworn vow to the Crown, as far as the British government was concerned.

The INA fought hard but the Japanese could not provide adequate help. Nevertheless, along with the Japanese army, the INA reached Imphal in Manipur, India by early 1944. Thereafter began the sad saga of retreat by the Japanese army, and in its train the INA, until the final surrender by Emperor Hirohito in August 1945.

Soon thereafter, Subhas, on his way from Taipei in Formosa (now Taiwan) was reported to have been killed in a plane crash. Whether this was true or not has not been adequately verified. Nevertheless, his call *Chalo Delhi ek saath Lal Qila dakhal karo* was fulfilled. His lieutenants Shah Nawaz Khan, Prem Sehgal and GS Dhillon were publicly tried in the Red Fort and acquitted.

In February, drawing from the example of the INA soldier, sailors of the Royal Indian Navy mutinied on the streets of Bombay (now Mumbai) as well as Karachi. This proved to be the final signal to Whitehall in London that the time of their holding on to the brightest jewel in the Crown of the British monarch was over. If so many soldiers and sailors, who had sworn by King and Country could break their vow, what was the guarantee that their civilian officers and men would remain loyal? And without them, how could the Crown rule India? London therefore decided to gracefully give India its freedom at the earliest.

In the last years, Gandhi had little to do with the fast-moving events. He listened to what Sardar Vallabhbhai Patel and Jawaharlal Nehru had to say. They conceded to the partition of the country. And he had to say yes, although in 1940 he had declared, 'Partition over my dead body'. Nevertheless, the credit for awakening the masses to the value of freedom must primarily go to Gandhi. But it was Netaji Subhas whose exploits made the dear British depart. The paradox is Gandhi is considered a greater contributor to India's freedom, not Subhas.

Living with Paradoxes

I

As is often stated, India is a unity in diversity. It is equally a variety in its paradoxes. Imagine another country whose Muslims were claimed to be a minority by their biggest leader in 1906 and thereafter many a concession obtained from the rulers on that criterion. In 1940, another great leader, popularly called the Qaid-e-Azam claimed that Muslims were a nation, distinct from other communities. On that ground alone, the rulers gave them a whole new country called Pakistan.

This was not the only contradiction within this paradox; there was another one. In 1906 the Muslim League was founded and thereafter it claimed to lead the community. The Congress refused to concede the point and claimed that it really was the leader of all Indians. The League was no great player, as was reflected by the results of the 1937 elections under the Government of India Act of 1935. Come the 1945-

46 general elections, the Muslim League won all the central seats and most of the provincial ones. These results convinced the British rulers that the Muslims wanted Pakistan and had to have it. Yet, the Congress leaders denied that it was a religious division of the country and continued to claim that they still had the following of many a Muslim. In fact, on the eve of his assassination in 1948, Gandhi told Dr Syama Prasad Mookerji and Dr Rajkumari Amrit Kaur that the partition was only a territorial division.

Till today, Hindu-Muslim clashes on the streets of the subcontinent are not unknown. Moreover, for half the weekdays, there are agitated television debates on this or that issue, whether the Hindus are right or the Muslims are correct. Whether a Ram Temple should be built in Ayodhya or should it not be built ? There is no doubt that an Islamic structure stood on the same spot in that holy town, where an imposing temple existed before, so opined the Archaeological Survey of India. Poet Allama Iqbal had called Ram 'Imam-e Hind' and he is known for being one of the prophets of Pakistan, especially after the 1930 plenary session of the Muslim League at Prayagraj (then Allahabad).

The paradox doesn't end here; it goes further. The Shia Muslims have openly conceded that the Ram Mandir should be built without any compensation to the Shias; incidentally, Qaid-e-Azam Jinnah, the founder of Pakistan was at birth and till his death, a Shia. But the Sunni leaders in India are squarely opposed to the Ram Mandir.

II

Since the general elections of 1957, some opposition parties have regularly alleged that the Congress indulges its policies that appeal to the Muslims and call this action 'votebank politics'. What they mean is that the Congress has been pampering the Muslim voters by serving them with manifestos which would reassure the community that its interests are closest to the party's heart. The motive is to ensure that Muslims keep voting for the Congress to ensure its success at the polls. There is no doubt that they respond positively, and they are a rewarding community to pamper. Their numbers may not be the largest but are large enough and they vote with a solemn sense of devotion to the ballot box. Being a well-knit community and generally obedient to their *ulema* or clergy, Muslims vote in unison, at least across a State. At voting time, they queue up before the booth and up to 90 per cent or more of them cast their ballot. This is invaluable, especially when the other communities do not vote in such great numbers nor in unison.

In the years when the rest did not cast their votes beyond 40 or 45 per cent, a Muslim vote amounted to more than two votes, not only because 45 × 2=90, but most of the Muslim votes went to a single candidate. If nothing else, this was a community of lesser numbers going all out to match the bigger numbers of the majority community and hoping to insist on its viewpoint being lent a ear. This was the thesis of a situation and continues to be so in every election. Yet, the opposition parties concerned about this are not seen to take steps, except protesting loudly that the Congress 'plays vote bank politics'.

The antithesis is clearly compulsory voting, as is practiced in Australia. If anything nearing a 100 per cent vote is cast, no minority vote, however prolific, can win. This is the ignored synthesis.

Glossary

Badshah	ruler
Bidi	a local cigerette
Dhoti	a wraparound
Divankhana	sitting room
Doab	the area between the rivers Ganges and Yamuna
Dohai	an excuse
Gherao	surroended by workers as a mark of protest
Islam-e-Jamhuriya	Islamic republic
Kar seva/ Karsevak	a religious duty of labour/ those who perform this holy duty
Mahatma	a great soul
Maulvi	religious teacher
Mohajirs	Muslims of interior India who migrated to Pakistan during Partition
Nizam-e-Mustafa	land of Sharia law
Paigambar	Prophet
Paramatma	The universal supreme being
Raees	a rich person
Rishi	asetics
Sadhu-Sanyasi	an hermit/an ascetic
Sahib	A British/ an upper class person
Ummah	community